HOW TO TAKE
GOOD PICTURES

HOW TO TAKE
GOOD PICTURES

A PHOTO GUIDE BY **Kodak**

An all new edition of the world's
best-selling photography book

HOW TO TAKE
GOOD PICTURES

Library of Congress Catalog Number: 81-66172
ISBN 0-345-29745-8

Manufactured in the United States of America
34th Edition, First 1981 Printing

9 8 7 6 5 4 3 2 1

CONTRIBUTORS
Eastman Kodak Company
  Martin L. Taylor, Author
  Donald S. Buck, Photography
  Neil Montanus, Photography

Mark Hobson, Photography
William Paris, Photo Research and Art Direction
Quarto Marketing Ltd., Design
Roger Pring and Christopher Meehan, Designers
Ken Diamond, Design Assistant

Table of Contents

INTRODUCTION

Photography offers a twofold thrill to picture-takers. There's the delight in the event that you are planning to capture, and there's the pleasure in reviewing the pictures days, weeks, or even years later. With a little confidence in your knowledge, skill, and experience, you'll find that arranging or discovering a photogenic scene provides great satisfaction. Pictures are reminders, keys to the past—even bits of history, personal or documentary. They also express your moods, impressions, and feelings of the moment—visible statements of a very personal art.

How to Take Good Pictures will help you improve your pictures with any kind of camera. The advice on the following pages will familiarize you with many basic elements and techniques of photography. And as you become better acquainted with the principles of successful picture-taking, you'll feel more confidence in your own results.

How to Take Good Pictures gives instruction with pictures, rather than with columns of number- and formula-laden text. In this step-by-step primer, words serve to emphasize or clarify the messages offered by the illustrations. The book begins with basic ideas for picture improvement and moves on to advanced concepts. Start with the Ten Top Techniques for Better Pictures on the next 8 pages. Then, either read on in sequence or turn to those sections that interest you the most.

Keeping a ready camera and searching for the best viewpoint can pay rich rewards, as in this view of Mont St. Michel. Notice how the peaceful grazing sheep help to establish distance relationships. Muted light from cloudy skies gives a special mood.

THE TEN TOP TECHNIQUES FOR BETTER PICTURES

(If you read no further, these ideas will give your picture-taking a dramatic improvement.)

1

Move close to your subject. Whether it is a New England church, the Matterhorn, or a child with ice cream, get close enough so that you see only the most important elements in the viewfinder. Failure to observe this simple guideline accounts for more unsuccessful pictures than any other photo mistake.

2

Make sure that your automatic or manually adjustable camera is adjusted to give correct exposure. If your pictures are too light or too dark, check the camera manual and the film instructions. Remember to set the film speed (ISO, ASA, or DIN number) on most automatic cameras and sometimes the shutter speed or the aperture. On a manually operated camera, set the film speed, shutter speed, and aperture.

Correct exposure

Overexposed

Underexposed

11

3

Carefully observe both background and foreground in your viewfinder before you take the picture. Clutter or confusing elements tend to dilute the strength of your subject. Keep your pictures as simple as possible.

Cluttered background

Simple background

4

Correctly exposed flash pictures must be made within the flash-to-subject distance range for snapshot cameras. For automatic or manually adjustable cameras, the distance determines any adjustments to be made.

Flash is for dark places.

5

Hold your camera steady. Shaky hands or punching the shutter-release button may give you fuzzy pictures. Brace the camera with both hands against your forehead and smoothly press the shutter release.

Shaky camera, fuzzy pictures.

Steady camera, sharp pictures.

6

Become thoroughly familiar with your camera. Read the instruction manual carefully so that you'll be comfortable making adjustments under a wide variety of conditions. As you read the manual, keep your camera in hand for reference.

Read your camera manual thoroughly.

Try putting your subject off center.

7

Set your subject slightly off-center. When shown dead-center in a picture, your subject may appear static and rather dull. Experiment to see where different subjects look best. Some cameras take square pictures and others take rectangular ones. If your camera takes rectangular pictures, you can get both horizontal and vertical pictures by holding the camera flat or on end.

8

Rather than posing people in a starchy, uncomfortable manner, engage them in a natural, absorbing activity to take their eyes off you and the camera. When people are doing something familiar, their bodies and faces will relax. The couple below was posed, of course, but the picture-taker found a way to draw their attention and commemorate a holiday at the same time.

Keep people occupied.

9

Watch the direction of light in your scene. People tend to squint in bright, direct light and the dark shadows are often unattractive. Light from the side or from behind your subject may be more effective than light from the front. Picture-taking in the shade or on an overcast day may be better, too, if it is possible with your camera.

Frontlighting—light from the front

Backlighting—light from behind

10

Take plenty of pictures. Every professional knows that the potential for success rises with the number of pictures taken. Compared with some of the rare scenes you'll encounter, film is far less expensive than the prospect of a missed opportunity.

OPERATING YOUR CAMERA

TYPES OF CAMERAS

All cameras provide the same function—to allow a measured quantity of light to strike film. The light makes an image on the film and you get a picture. If you have an instant-print camera and film, you get a finished print from the camera. If you have a conventional camera that takes black-and-white, color negative, or color slide film, the film must be processed by a photofinisher. You get slides or prints and negatives.

In this book, we'll discuss the use of several camera types: instant-print, cartridge-loading, and 35 mm. These cameras all work in basically the same way. Their topography may be slightly different, but the controls perform similar functions. In the next few pages, we'll provide a thumbnail sketch of each camera type, including its assets and its operating procedures. Since some cameras are more complex than others, we'll devote more space to them for greater clarity.

We'll be showing and describing some current cameras in this section. No matter what camera you have, you'll want to refer to the instruction manual for specific information on loading and operating procedures. Kodak can furnish a replacement manual for a Kodak camera if your manual has disappeared. The same may be true with other manufacturers. Try your photo dealer if information for your camera is unavailable. Dealers are familiar with many cameras and should be happy to help.

INSTANT CAMERAS

Most instant cameras are delightfully easy to use. Flash operation differs from model to model, and a few models may need to be focused, but generally there is little to learn and less to fuss with.

Advantages Instant cameras are great when you want to see your pictures right away. Parties and gatherings of all types are natural situations. Travel and vacations are fun with instant cameras, because you can send instant prints instead of post cards. Anyone with children will appreciate the instant results when taking pictures of youthful antics. The kids love them.

The beauty of instant photography lies in the complete picture that arrives only minutes after you snap the shutter. Share exciting photos with friends, party guests, travel acquaintances, and amused family members. Send prints to penpals and relatives. Get even more mileage from your instant efforts when you order copyprints from your photofinisher.

Operation As mentioned above, there's not much to using an instant camera. You'll want to know how to load and unload your camera, how to make any adjustments, and how to operate the flash. Picture-taking usually starts with loading the camera. Here's how to load a KODAK Instant Camera. (You might start at the right, with unloading, just in case you're faced with a camera that has an empty pack of film inside.)

Unloading

If the film-counting window shows "0" or plain black, the camera is out of film and needs to be reloaded.

Loading

1. Holding the film pack by the edges only, remove the new print-film pack from the wrapping material.

4. Now the film-counting window will show a white square with a black dot in the center.

2. Then insert it into the film compartment by lining up the stripe on the pack with the loading line on the camera.

3. Slide the film into the back of the compartment and close the door so that it latches securely.

5. Press the shutter release and allow it to return to eject the protective black plastic film cover from the new pack.

1. Open the film-compartment door by pressing the film-compartment latch.

2. If needed, remove the empty film pack by pulling the film-pack extractor and withdrawing the spent pack.

6. The number "1" should appear in the film-counting window. You're ready to take a picture.

7. Set the lighten/darken control at the center position. (If a picture looks too dark or too light, you can improve it with the lighten/darken control.)

21

Adjustments

The KODAK Instant Cameras shown on these pages have automatic exposure control that adjusts the camera for the lighting conditions. If a red light appears in the viewfinder, use flash or place the camera on a firm support for a time exposure.

If a print is a little too dark or light, use the *lighten/darken* control to correct your next print.

Some models have a lens that requires focusing. You may have to estimate the distance and set the focusing control accordingly. Or you may set the focus with the help of visual aids in the viewfinder. On others, you can make an adjustment to take close-up pictures.

Special Conditions

In extremely hot weather keep the camera and film as cool as conveniently possible. Developing prints come out best if allowed to develop in the shade.

In extremely cold weather, keep the cameras as warm as possible. For best results, place a developing print in an inside, warm pocket as soon as it leaves the camera.

Flash

Flash is a simple matter with instant cameras. There are two approaches. Some cameras have a built-in electronic flash, and others accept disposable flash devices or detachable electronic flash units. Whatever the case, flash will give you enough light for a 4- to 10-foot range from the camera. You merely turn on the flash or attach the correct flash device for your camera and take a picture. Electronic flash units take a while to warm up. There is a little indicator light, which must be on or blinking that shows that the flash is ready for use. After each picture, wait for the light to glow.

If your instant camera has a built-in flash like this, you slide it to one side to turn it on.

Other instant cameras may accept an accessory electronic flash unit. The unit clips on to the top of the camera and locks to the side of the camera with a screw. You turn it on by sliding it to the side.

Some instant cameras also accept disposable flash sources such as this flipflash. Insert a fresh flipflash and take flash pictures. When all the flash cells on top have been fired, flip the unit over and insert the other end to use the fresh cells.

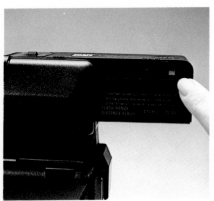

Whatever electronic flash system you have, wait for the ready light to glow before taking a picture.

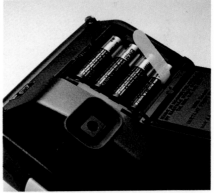

When the recycle time of an electronic flash unit is longer than recommended (the ready light takes a long time to glow), change the batteries.

23

CARTRIDGE-LOADING CAMERAS

Cartridge-loading cameras are perhaps the simplest to operate of all conventional film cameras. Loading is easy, and there are few if any adjustments to be made.

The small, 110-size cartridge fits in pocket cameras. The larger 126 cartridge fits in the familiar KODAK INSTAMATIC ® cameras.

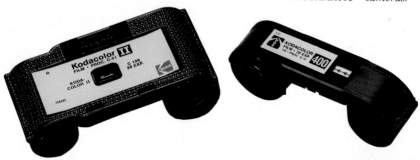

Advantages Cartridge-loading cameras—particularly the 110 size—are small and lightweight so that they're easy to pack around. Although you have to send the film to be processed, you will have a great variety of processing services available. Print quality is superb in most situations and the cost of the camera is usually fairly low.

The simplest of all cartridge-loading cameras give the greatest ease of operation. There is nothing to do except load the film and snap a picture. You can take pictures on sunny days or hazy days outdoors, or use flash for nearby subjects when the light is dim.

More advanced models, which naturally cost more, may adapt to a wider range of lighting conditions. Not only can you take pictures in bright conditions, but you can also take pictures under heavy overcast or in the shade. Some cameras even allow you to take pictures without flash in the typical light of your home.

Operation Picture-taking with a cartridge-loading camera is easy and fun. Loading is usually the first step. Let's take a look. (Again, we'll first show unloading in case your camera contains a completely exposed cartridge of film and your instruction manual has disappeared.)

Unloading 110 Cameras

If you see a cartridge with an empty center window, or no cartridge at all in your 110-size camera, it's time to reload.

Open the film-compartment door by sliding the latch.

Drop the cartridge out in your hand.

Unloading 126 Cameras

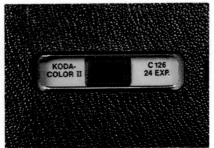

When you see an empty film-cartridge window or no cartridge at all in a 126-size camera, it's time to reload.

Open the film-compartment door by depressing the latch at the side of the camera. Swing the door open.

Drop the cartridge into your hand.

25

Loading 110 Cameras

1. Remove the wrapping from the new cartridge, and insert it into the camera. It will fit only one way.

2. Close the film-compartment door and slide the latch to make sure that the door is locked.

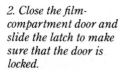

3. Advance the film by sliding the advance lever into the camera several times.

4. When the number "1" appears in the cartridge window and the advance lever moves no farther, you're ready to take pictures.

Loading 126 Cameras

1. Unwrap the cartridge. Insert it into the camera. It fits only one way.

2. Close the film-compartment door.

3. Advance the film with the advance lever until the number "1" shows in the cartridge window. The film-advance lever will move no farther.

Adjustments

There are few adjustments to be made on most cartridge-loading cameras. (If you have an older cartridge-loading camera which requires that you set aperture and shutter speed, refer to the setting instructions for 35 mm cameras on page 36.) The most sophisticated of these cameras are automatic and include exposure meters that tell the camera how to set itself for the prevailing light conditions.

Less sophisticated models lack some of the useful exposure capability of the more expensive models, but can give excellent pictures within a slightly narrower lighting range.

Some cartridge-loading cameras, particularly cameras with optional telephoto lenses and older models may have a focusing control. You focus by estimating the distance between you and the subject and making the appropriate setting. Or you move the focusing control and watch for the sharp focus indicator in the viewfinder.

On some cartridge-loading cameras you may focus the camera with a lever on top of the camera. Some cameras require that you estimate the camera-to-subject distance. On others, you'll see a focusing cue in the viewfinder.

When you look at a subject in the viewfinder of a focusing camera, the center spot may show two images side by side. If you snap the shutter, the resulting picture may be fuzzy.

By moving the focusing control on top of the camera, you align the two images in the center of the viewfinder, and the entire scene will appear sharp. The resulting picture should also be sharp.

Film

Cartridge-loading cameras accept films for color and black-and-white prints and color slides. Kodak offers color films with different sensitivity to light. A sensitive or high-speed film will let you take pictures in darker conditions than with a less sensitive film. A more sensitive film may also extend the flash range of your camera. Ask your photo dealer for film recommendations when you make your next purchase, and see page 46 for more information on film. (Slide films are not recommended for many cameras using 110 cartridges.)

Flash

Flash is easy with cartridge-loading cameras. Some cameras have built-in electronic flash. Others need to have a flash device inserted. Attachable electronic flash units are usually available, as well as disposable devices such as flipflash, magicubes, or flashcubes. With a camera that has a built-in electronic flash, you merely turn on the flash and wait for the ready light to glow. Then you're ready to take a picture. After you've taken a picture, you must wait for the light to glow again before you take the next picture.

If you have a camera with an attachable electronic flash unit, the same guidelines apply. Attach the flash unit. Turn the unit on. Wait for the ready light to glow, and then take a picture. Take the next

Many cartridge-loading cameras accept an accessory electronic flash unit. You insert it into the slot that accepts disposable flash devices, and tighten the clamp that holds the bottom of the camera. A switch on the side of the unit turns it on. Wait for the ready light to glow before taking a picture.

picture after the ready light glows again.

All electronic flash units work on batteries. Replace the batteries as soon as the time required for the ready light to glow between pictures exceeds the number of seconds suggested in the instruction manual.

The flash range for good pictures for most of these cameras with any type of flash is in the 4 to 12-foot range, usually marked on the camera. Subjects nearer than that will be overexposed and washed out in your pictures. Subjects farther away will be underexposed—too dark. By using a more sensitive film, you can extend the flash range to 18 feet or more.

A new cartridge-loading camera may have a built-in electronic flash unit that turns on automatically when the camera senses a dark scene. The red light comes on when dark lighting conditions require flash. The green light comes on when the flash is ready. Older models may have a switch.

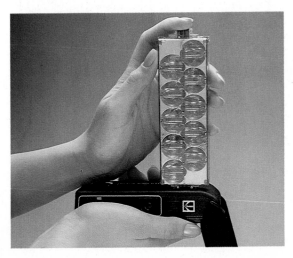

Insert a disposable flash device such as a flipflash into the top of the camera for convenient flash pictures. When you have fired all the flash cells on one side, turn the flash over to use the fresh cells on the other side.

35 mm CAMERAS

There are dozens of current 35 mm cameras, and probably hundreds of older cameras. They fall into two basic groups—reflex and rangefinder. Rangefinder cameras are smaller, less expensive, and somewhat less flexible than the reflex variety. Many reflex cameras can be fitted with a warehouse of accessories that will give every photographic effect imaginable.

These cameras usually cost more than instant-print or cartridge-loading cameras because they're quite a bit more capable. For the extra cost, you get the capability to take pictures more precisely in a wide range of lighting conditions. The combination of manual or automatic exposure control, a selection of shutter speeds and apertures, and a great variety of general and special-purpose films allow you to photograph whatever you choose and in almost any circumstance.

To keep things simple, we'll divide 35 mm cameras into two groups, reflex and rangefinder. Many non-reflex cameras do not have rangefinder focusing, but share most other features with true rangefinder cameras.

Operation Operating a 35 mm camera requires a bit of understanding for best results. We'll give enough basic information in this section to get you started with your 35 mm camera. For a better understanding of how photography works, and how such information applies to you and your 35 mm camera, turn to page 124. That section of the book will clarify questions about settings. There's also information on flash, filters, and other subjects that will help you make better pictures in a variety of situations.

The obvious place to start our description of 35 mm operation is with film loading. (A camera that hasn't been used recently may have exposed film inside. The first step, then, will be unloading.)

Rangefinder cameras are typically automated so that you merely load film into the camera, set the film speed, focus (although some cameras have automatic focusing), and take a picture. Many reflex cameras are completely automatic and with others you adjust one element of the exposure setting so that the camera can make the other. Vintage cameras may be completely manual.

Unloading 35 mm Cameras

If your camera has made the last exposure on a magazine of film, depress the film-advance release button on the bottom of the camera.

Pull out the rewind lever, and turn it in the direction indicated until you feel no more resistance.

Open the film-compartment door by sliding a latch on the back or side of the camera or by pulling up the rewind lever.

Remove the film magazine by pulling up the rewind lever, if necessary, and dropping the magazine in your hand.

Loading 35 mm Cameras

Insert a new film magazine into the film compartment. The edge of the leader strip with the sprocket holes should be at the bottom. Press the rewind lever down to lock the magazine in position. Hook a sprocket hole into the film take-up spool. Advance the film until both sets of sprocket holes are riding on the sprockets.

Close the film-compartment door so that it snaps shut.

Advance the film and snap the shutter several times until the number "1" shows in the film-counting window.

33

Exposure with Automatic and Semi-Automatic Cameras

All automatic 35 mm cameras and cameras with built-in exposure meters have one exposure adjustment in common—the film-speed setting. When you load a roll of film into the camera, always check the film-speed setting and reset it, if necessary. Many new rangefinder cameras make all the other exposure adjustments themselves without any help from you. With older rangefinder models and many reflex cameras, you set either aperture or shutter speed—the camera then measures the light on the scene and makes the other setting.

You're expected to understand the reasons for choosing one setting over another. You may not understand now, but you want to get out and begin taking pictures. You can learn as you go along. At this point, we'll give you enough information to start taking good pictures, but for a fuller enjoyment of your camera, read the sections on exposure and depth of field starting on page 134.

Shutter-Speed Preferred If your camera is shutter-speed preferred, you choose the shutter speed and the camera chooses the aperture. A general

Set the film speed of the film you're using on the film-speed selector.

A shutter speed of 1/125 second (125 on the shutter speed dial) is excellent for general picture-taking with a medium-speed film.

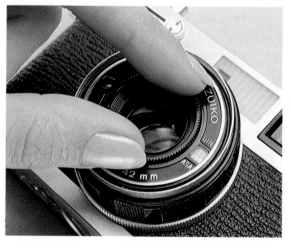

shutter speed for most daylight conditions is 1/125 second, represented by the number 125 on the shutter speed dial. When you're photographing a fast-moving subject in fairly bright light, try 1/250 second (250 on the shutter speed dial). In case the lighting conditions get so dim that you can't take a picture, try a shutter speed of 1/30 second (30).

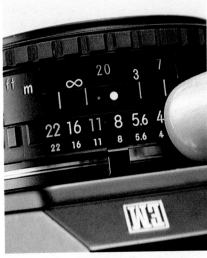

Aperture Preferred If your automatic camera is aperture preferred, you choose the aperture and the camera chooses the shutter speed. For most daylight picture-taking with a general-purpose film (ISO/ASA 64-200), you can set the aperture ring to *f*/8 and expect fine results. If the light becomes substantially dimmer, use larger apertures. (The larger the aperture, the smaller the number—*f*/4 might be a good choice for a dark day with an ISO/ASA 64-200 speed film.) In very dark surroundings, use the largest aperture available. At the beach or on snow in bright sunlight, use a small aperture such as *f*/16.

An aperture-preferred automatic camera requires that you set the aperture; the camera sets the shutter speed for the lighting conditions. First, make sure that the correct film speed is set on the camera. Then, set the aperture. A good aperture for general picture-taking is f/8.

Manual Cameras

Many 35 mm cameras are not automatic. Most are quite simple to operate. The majority have built-in exposure meters that help you make appropriate settings for the lighting conditions and for the film you're using.

Some cameras give you exposure information in the viewfinder. You may see the shutter speed set on the camera and the aperture set on the lens. Visual cues such as a set of LEDs or LCDs or a needle in a bracket will tell you when the settings will give good exposure. When the meter is turned on, the viewfinder display becomes active. Adjusting either the shutter speed dial or the lens aperture ring, or both, will center the needle in its bracket or light the correct LED or LCD.

Older cameras may have the visual cues on the outside of the camera. You point the camera at the subject and adjust the camera until the cue—usually a needle—is centered in the bracket. The meter window is often found on top of the camera. You read the suggested shutter speed and aperture settings from this window and transfer the information to the shutter speed dial and the lens aperture ring.

There are cameras that are completely manual—there is no built-in meter. You may have a separate, handheld meter that will help you determine the settings for a well-exposed picture. With most meters you merely aim the meter at the subject, turn on the meter, and read the recommended settings from the meter dial. You may have to transfer a value indicated by the meter needle to a scale that will show you all the possible exposure combinations of shutter speed and lens aperture.

No matter what kind of exposure meter you're using, two things are critical—setting the correct film speed on the meter and operating it according to the manufacturer's instructions. Write the manufacturer for instructions, if you don't have them, or ask your photo dealer for help.

Instructions *If you have an adjustable camera with no exposure meter, try the exposure combinations listed in the table at right. In each box the bold combination is the most logical choice. Other combinations are listed for your convenience and for special situations. (See pages 135 and 136.) For darker conditions, refer to the existing light exposure table on page 162. Shutter speeds slower than 1/30 second, have not been included in this table because they require steady support for the camera, such as a tripod. Notice that film speed varies the combinations of settings shown in the table. Film is available for 35 mm cameras in different sensitivities. Very sensitive film (ISO/ASA 160 to 400) is for dim lighting conditions. Other, less sensitive films are best in normal lighting.*

Outdoor Settings for a Manual Camera

Film Speed ISO/ASA	Light Conditions				
	Bright or Hazy Sun on Light Sand or Snow	Bright or Hazy Sun (Distinct Shadows)	Weak Hazy Sun (Soft Shadows)	Cloudy Bright (No Shadows)	Open Shade or Heavy Overcast
25-32	1/125, f/11 1/60, f/16 1/30, f/22 1/250, f/8 1/500, f/5.6 1/1000, f/4	1/125, f/8 1/60, f/11 1/30, f/16 1/250, f/5.6 1/500, f/4 1/1000, f/2.8	1/125, f/5.6 1/60, f/8 1/30, f/11 1/250, f/4 1/500, f/2.8 1/1000, f/2	1/125, f/4 1/60, f/5.6 1/30, f/8 1/250, f/2.8 1/500, f/2 1/1000, f/1.4	1/60, f/4 1/30, f/5.6 1/125, f/2.8 1/250, f/2 1/500, f/1.4
64	1/125, f/16 1/60, f/22 1/250, f/11 1/500, f/8 1/1000, f/5.6	1/125, f/11 1/60, f/16 1/30, f/22 1/250, f/8 1/500, f/5.6 1/1000, f/4	1/125, f/8 1/60, f/11 1/30, f/16 1/250, f/5.6 1/500, f/4 1/1000, f/2.8	1/125, f/5.6 1/60, f/8 1/30, f/11 1/250, f/4 1/500, f/2.8 1/1000, f/2	1/125, f/4 1/60, f/5.6 1/30, f/8 1/250, f/2.8 1/500, f/2 1/1000, f/1.4
100-125*	1/125, f/16 1/60, f/22 1/250, f/11 1/500, f/8 1/1000, f/5.6	1/125, f/11 1/60, f/16 1/30, f/22 1/250, f/8 1/500, f/5.6 1/1000, f/4	1/125, f/8 1/60, f/11 1/30, f/16 1/250, f/5.6 1/500, f/4 1/1000, f/2.8	1/125, f/5.6 1/60, f/8 1/30, f/11 1/250, f/4 1/500, f/2.8 1/1000, f/2	1/125, f/4 1/60, f/5.6 1/30, f/8 1/250, f/2.8 1/500, f/2 1/1000, f/1.4
200	1/500, f/16 1/250, f/22 1/1000, f/11	1/250, f/16 1/125, f/22 1/500, f/11 1/1000, f/8	1/250, f/11 1/125, f/16 1/60, f/22 1/500, f/8 1/1000, f/5.6	1/250, f/8 1/125, f/11 1/60, f/16 1/30, f/22 1/500, f/5.6 1/1000, f/4	1/250, f/5.6 1/125, f/8 1/60, f/11 1/30, f/16 1/500, f/4 1/1000, f/2.8
400 slide	1/1000, f/16 1/500, f/22	1/500, f/16 1/250, f/22 1/1000, f/11	1/500, f/11 1/250, f/16 1/125, f/22 1/1000, f/8	1/500, f/8 1/250, f/11 1/125, f/16 1/60, f/22 1/1000, f/5.6	1/500, f/5.6 1/250, f/8 1/125, f/11 1/60, f/16 1/30, f/22 1/1000, f/4
400 neg*	1/500, f/16 1/250, f/22 1/1000, f/11	1/500, f/11 1/250, f/16 1/125, f/22 1/1000, f/8	1/500, f/8 1/250, f/11 1/125, f/16 1/60, f/22 1/1000, f/5.6	1/250, f/8 1/125, f/11 1/60, f/16 1/30, f/22 1/500, f/5.6 1/1000, f/4	1/250, f/5.6 1/125, f/8 1/60, f/11 1/30, f/16 1/500, f/4 1/1000, f/2.8

*Negative films tolerate overexposure. Overexpose them up to one full stop for safety. Slide films, however, must be exposed accurately.

Focusing

If you have a completely automatic camera, either rangefinder or reflex, you need only focus the camera to take a picture. There are generally two systems for focusing. With the simpler, you estimate the distance between you and your subject and set that distance in feet or as indicated by the appropriate symbol on the camera lens. More advanced systems allow you to view the subject through the viewfinder and turn the focusing ring on the lens until a visual cue tells you that the lens is focused. Since focusing varies from camera to camera, it's wise to consult your instruction manual. Some cameras now have an automatic focusing device that does all the work for you. You point the camera at your subject, press the shutter release, and you've taken a sharp picture.

Flash

Electronic flash is the most common source of portable light with 35 mm cameras. It is convenient and compact and provides a way for you to take pictures when there isn't enough light.

Many rangefinder cameras have a small electronic flash unit built into the camera. To take a flash picture you extend the flash unit and turn it on. When the ready light glows, you take a picture. You must wait for the ready light to glow again before taking the next picture. Occasionally, you will have to replace the separate batteries that power the flash. You can tell that the batteries are ready for retirement when the ready light takes

Many nonreflex cameras have a built-in electronic flash unit. Slide or depress a switch to turn it on. For a sharp, correctly exposed picture, set the camera-to-subject distance on the lens. When the orange ready light glows, you're ready to take a picture.

longer to glow than the instruction manual recommends. Although focusing the camera on your subject sets the camera for flash exposure, check the manual for the flash range that will give you good pictures.

Other rangefinder and reflex cameras are equipped so that you can attach an auxiliary flash unit. A shoe on the top of the camera will accept the foot of most flash units. The first step is to insert the flash unit into the shoe. If the accessory shoe and flash foot are "hot" (check the camera instruction manual), all the necessary electrical connections have been made by inserting the flash unit. If the flash shoe or foot isn't hot, you make the electrical connection with a small cord (the PC cord) usually supplied with the flash unit. Plug the cord into the flash and into the correct socket on the camera and you're in business. Set the camera shutter speed as recommended by the camera instruction manual for correct shutter synchronization. A typical synchronization setting for electronic flash would be 1/60 or 1/125 second.

Newer cameras usually have an electrically wired accessory shoe on top of the camera. When you slide a similarly wired flash unit into the shoe, all the electrical connections are established. Older cameras or older flash units may require the use of a small cord that comes with the flash unit to make the connection.

Flash Exposure

Setting the aperture depends on the flash-to-subject distance. Generally, there are three systems for choosing the aperture, which we'll discuss in more detail in the "Flash" section of the book, page 150—self-quenching automatic, dedicated, and manual. Self-quenching automatic means that the flash unit has a sensor that shuts off the flash when enough light has reached the subject. First, you set the film speed on the flash unit. Then choose an aperture/distance-range mode and set the recommended aperture on the camera for that mode. To take a picture, you focus, make sure that the subject is in the distance range for that flash mode, and snap the shutter.

Automatic flash units require that you set the film speed on the calculator on the back of the flash unit. Then choose an automatic flash mode for the distances you'll be photographing. Here we chose the yellow mode. Set the aperture—f/8 in this case—recommended by the flash unit. Make sure that the distance between flash and subject falls within the automatic flash range—1.6 to 8.5 feet in this case.

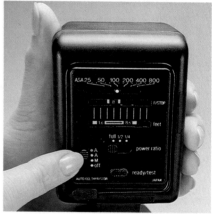

Dedicated flash systems differ, but the idea is generally the same. A sensor in the camera (not on the flash) determines when enough light has reached the film, and then shuts off the power in the flash unit. Since these systems vary, you'll want to pay careful attention to the instructions. Some rangefinder cameras allow you to set the guide number of the flash (a number found in the flash instruction manual that describes the power of the unit with a specific film) on the camera. When you set the camera to a flash mode, you select the aperture by focusing the camera.

A dedicated flash and camera system will establish all connections when the flash is attached.

40

Manual flash is easier to talk about but takes a few more steps to perform. When the flash is all connected to the camera, you set the film speed on the flash calculator, and focus on the subject. Refer to the distance scale on the lens barrel for the camera-to-subject distance. Then apply that distance to the flash calculator. The aperture number will appear across from the distance. Set the lens aperture and take a picture.

Set the recommended flash shutter speed on the camera. Then set the film speed on the flash calculator dial. Focus on your subject. The flash-to-subject distance will appear on the lens distance scale. Apply that distance to the flash calculator. Here it is 10 feet. The recommended aperture setting, here, between f/5.6 and f/8, will appear across from the flash-to-subject distance. Set the recommended aperture on the lens-aperture ring.

Electronic flash units work on either rechargeable batteries or disposable batteries. When the recycle times get longer than recommended by the flash manual, replace or recharge the batteries. For more important flash battery information, refer to page 155.

CAMERA HANDLING

Proper camera handling may be one of the most important contributions to good pictures. We have a number of tips to help you improve the way you take pictures.

Holding the Camera Steady
Start taking sharp pictures by holding the camera steady. Stand comfortably balanced with your legs slightly apart. Grip the camera, one hand on each side, and gently press your elbows into your side. If you've been exerting— walking up a mountain trail, for example—let your breathing resume a slow, steady pace before taking a picture.

Pressing the Shutter Release
Slowly press the shutter-release button until the camera takes a picture. This will give you a better chance at sharp pictures and help you maintain good composition.

Keeping the Lens Clear
One common problem is arranging a beautiful scene in the viewfinder only to discover later that a finger, the camera strap, part of the camera case, or even the lens cap covered the lens while you took a picture. Make it a practice to clear the lens area of obstructions before taking the picture.

Focusing

There are three typical focusing operations. The simplest is choosing one of several symbols on the distance scale on the lens that corresponds to the approximate distance between you and your subject. Or, you set the camera-to-subject distance in feet or metres.

Some cameras have a rangefinder coupled to the lens. To focus, you turn the lens focusing ring until the two images in the center of the viewfinder coincide. You can also set the calculated distance in feet or metres on the lens distance scale.

With automatic focusing, thoroughly digest the information in the camera instruction manual.

In a single-lens-reflex camera you can see when the lens is focused because you see the same image the lens sees. There are a number of aids to help you, usually found in the center portion of the viewfinder.

Using the Viewfinder

In some camera viewfinders, the picture area is defined by a bright rectangle or square. Other camera viewfinders use the entire viewfinder. Check your instruction manual to get the important elements of the scene into your picture.

When you see foreground litter or a confusing background in the viewfinder, choose another position. Horizons should be level.

Camera Support

Many automatic and adjustable cameras will operate at shutter speeds slower than 1/30 second. At these slow speeds, even your steadiest position, grip, and release may jiggle the camera and result in blurred pictures. Lean against a tree or wall or rest the camera on a table or rock. A tripod will give the most reliable steady support. A cable release will remove your shaky hands from the camera.

Using the Self-Timer

The self-timer is handy when you want to include yourself in the picture. Set the timer, press the shutter release, and position yourself in the picture. You'll have between 8 and 12 seconds to get there. When you're arranging the picture in the viewfinder, leave room for yourself. Place your camera on a solid support such as a table, fence post, rock, or tripod.

FILM

Film is available in different sizes for different cameras. Check your camera instruction manual for the correct size film. And, choose film for the kind of pictures you want—color prints, color slides, or black-and-white prints.

Films are also available with different sensitivities to light. "Fast" films are very sensitive. You might use them in dim light. There are also slower films that are good for very sharp pictures in bright light. You'll probably want to use a medium-speed film for most picture-taking.

The speed or sensitivity is identified by ISO, ASA, or DIN numbers. (These letters stand for different standard setting organizations. ISO/DIN values are common in Europe while ISO/ASA values are used in the US and England.) A medium-speed film might have an ISO/ASA rating of

110-size   box   cartridge   negative   print   camera

126-size   box   cartridge   negative   print   camera

64 to 125. Faster film would be 160 to 400, and a slower film 25 to 32.

Most films are manufactured to give pictures in daylight—the light from the sun. A few others, however, are designed to give pictures with correct color appearance when used with special light sources—household bulbs (tungsten) or photographic lights. See pages 133 and 166–167 for more information about these films.

There is an expiration date on most film packaging. Film can go bad, just like food, and when it does, you can get pictures of inferior quality. Check the date when you buy new film, and don't forget the film in your camera. Take the pictures and get them processed quickly. Film doesn't like extreme heat or humidity, either. Keep it out of direct sunlight and other hotspots.

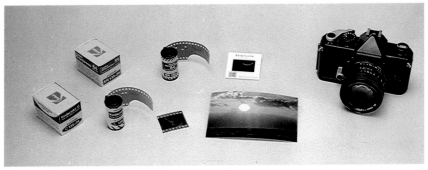

135-size   box   cassettes   negative   slide   print   camera

Instant   box   film pack   print   camera

PEOPLE

When you photograph people—friends and family or interesting strangers—you want them to look their best. Portray them naturally. Show some of the unique traits that distinguish them from the rest of the crowd. Spend a moment considering what important characteristics identify the people close to you. It might be helpful to suggest expressions, clothing, props, and activities that will encourage the real people to emerge from behind the snapshot smile-masks.

Direction of light

Frontlighting   *Sidelighting*   *Backlighting*

OUTDOORS

Light—its direction and intensity—is all-important in your outdoor portraits. Direct sunlight can illuminate a subject from one of three directions. *Frontlighting* is harsh, usually causing a person to squint, and often making heavy shadows on the person's face. *Sidelighting,* where half of the face is in shadow, can be effective for a dramatic portrayal. *Backlighting* will give a silhouette when the camera is adjusted for a sunlight exposure; it can give a gentle appearance, however, when the camera is adjusted to record the subject's most important features. (Backlighting can fool an automatic camera. See page 140.)

There are two ways to cope with direct, bright sunlight from any direction. One way is to place a piece of white cardboard in a position to reflect some light into the shadow areas. Almost anything in a light, neutral tone will do—bedsheets, a newspaper, towels, a white wall, or even a sidewalk.

Fill·in Flash

Fill-in flash can brighten dark shadows in outdoor pictures. A camera that has built-in flash or that takes disposable flash devices provides easy flash fill. Position your subject near the maximum distance recommended by the camera manual and take a flash picture.

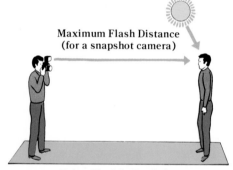

Maximum Flash Distance
(for a snapshot camera)

Using Flash in Daylight

If you have an adjustable or automatic camera that accepts an accessory flash, perform all the usual steps to take a flash picture (see pages 38 and 150–155. Set the camera for the sunlighted situation, but select a shutter speed that will synchronize with the flash—generally 1/60 or 1/125 second. A medium- or slow-speed film may be helpful. Then position your subject at a distance that will require more flash power than your flash unit can provide. You want the flash to fill the shadows subtly, not overpower the sunlight. See pages 158–159 for more on fill-in flash.

Overcast sky

From above

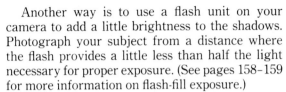

Another way is to use a flash unit on your camera to add a little brightness to the shadows. Photograph your subject from a distance where the flash provides a little less than half the light necessary for proper exposure. (See pages 158–159 for more information on flash-fill exposure.)

Light shade or overcast skies give more appealing pictures of people than direct sunlight. You'll get open, easy expressions without dark shadows. Since there's less light in these conditions, an automatic camera will automatically give more exposure. With a manual camera you'll have to make the necessary adjustment. (See pages 134–141.)

You can subtly change a person's appearance by changing the camera angle. A person photographed from above, a high angle, seems smaller and less important than someone photographed from below, a low camera angle. When the camera is aimed from eye level or a bit below, the effect is called normal. Most people prefer to be photographed at eye level. Be careful that an unusual camera angle doesn't distort your subject.

sunlight

below

At eye level

People wear natural expressions when they're occupied.

Look through the viewfinder at the entire scene. Make sure that no clutter in the background or foreground interferes with your view of the subject. Move in close to the person—close enough to keep only the essential features in the picture. (If using fill-in flash, move in only as far as good exposure will permit.) Another way to keep foreground and background simple is to change camera position and angle until you see exactly what you want in the viewfinder. You can also control depth of field so that the person is sharp and the rest of the scene is blurred. (See page 142.)

People wear natural expressions when they're comfortable. Try to have your subjects in relaxed positions—leaning against something or seated. When people have something to occupy their hands and attention, you'll get authentic portraits. Make sure your model is wearing clothing he or she finds appropriate and that is acceptable to your eye for color, coordination, and neatness.

Depth of field

Large aperture—f/2 *Small aperture—f/22*

Window light

Tungsten light

INDOORS

Most of the outdoor guidelines apply to making effective portraits indoors. You want people to be comfortable, relaxed, and to appear in pictures as they do in day-to-day life. Seated comfortably in a pleasant spot with an attractive, simple background is one answer. An alternative is to engage your subject in an activity that is interesting, familiar, and appropriate, such as a hobby or sport.

Again, lighting is important. You'll find four possible sources for indoor light: existing light from outdoors shining through a window or a door, artificial light given by tungsten or fluorescent bulbs, flash, and strong tungsten bulbs in reflectors called photolamps. (See next page.)

Flash

Window light reflected from book

Existing Light The existing light* looks best, of course, whether it's from the outdoors or from artificial sources such as household lamps. If you use light from the outside, move your subject close to a window or doorway, positioned so that lighting on the face is even and so that your picture will not include much of the bright window or doorway. The bright area could fool an exposure meter or automatic camera into underexposing the subject's face. A reflector can brighten the shadows caused by light from a single direction.

Taking pictures by household lamps requires fast film (ISO/ASA 400), slow shutter speeds (1/60 second or less) and wide apertures (f/2.8 or larger) because normal home lighting is much darker than daylight. Pose people near bright light

Using Photolamps

Create effective lighting with photolamps. Bulbs and reflectors are sold by photo, hardware, and electrical dealers. One lamp, reflecting off a wall, will give a pleasing portrait. Three lamps give many lighting possibilities. Using an exposure meter or an automatic camera should give good exposure.

Using a single lamp.

sources, but don't include those lights in your picture. Try to have the lighting as even as possible on the person's face. When the lighting is extremely dim and you need a shutter speed slower than 1/30 second, mount your camera on a steady support such as a tripod for sharp pictures.

Tungsten bulbs give a different color light from daylight. Use a high-speed film designed for tungsten light or use daylight film with an 80A filter attached to the camera lens†. In fluorescent light, also a different color from daylight, use daylight film and a CC30M filter†. Otherwise, your pictures may have a greenish tint. If you use KODACOLOR 400 Film for color prints, you can expect good results without a filter.

*See pages 160–163 for more on existing light.
†See pages 164–175 for more on filters.

Three lamps.

Using An Exposure Meter

Many advanced automatic and adjustable cameras allow you to make some decisions about setting the camera for unusual lighting conditions. These cameras generally have a built-in exposure meter that either gives you advice on how to set the camera yourself or makes the adjustments for you. Older adjustable cameras may not have a built-in meter. If yours doesn't, you may know how to operate a handheld meter.

The best advice for using any camera with a built-in meter or any handheld meter is to get as close as possible to the subject to make a meter reading. Make your settings as the meter indicates from the close-up position. If the camera is automatic, there is usually some way to override the automatic setting feature in unusual exposure situations. Take a meter reading close to the subject and then back off to your preferred camera position. Adjust the camera manually to keep the exposure settings recommended by the meter at the close position. For a better understanding of exposure, see pages 134–141. For better understanding of how your particular camera operates, check the instruction manual.

Flash Flash, of course, is one of the most popular sources for light in dark places. Electronic flash units are available for most cameras, and the cost per flash is very low. Many units are automatic within certain distance ranges, allowing sufficient exposure without further adjustment. As with photolamps, a single flash will provide enough

Flash Pictures

Flash photography is easy with nearly any camera. Most snapshot cameras are equipped for an attachable flash device such as a flip-flash or an accessory electronic flash unit. Some snapshot cameras have built-in electronic flash. Attach and/or turn on the flash device or unit; make sure that your subject is in the flash distance range, and take a picture. Allow the ready light on an electronic flash unit to glow before you take the next picture.

With 35 mm cameras that have built-in flash, you turn the flash on, focus the camera if necessary, and take a picture. Adjustable or automatic cameras that accept accessory flash units may require some adjustment. Some dedicated systems may need to have a particular aperture set on the camera. More sophisticated dedicated systems may need other settings.

Automatic, self-quenching flash units operate in several distance ranges at different aperture settings, depending on film speed. Determine the typical distance you'll be photographing, and choose the appropriate mode on the flash unit. The unit usually requires a specific aperture setting for each flash mode.

With a manual flash you set the film speed on the calculator on the back of the flash unit, then focus on the subject. Look at the lens distance scale to find out camera-to-subject distance. Refer to the flash calculator dial and find the aperture to set on your camera—it will be approximately across from the camera-to-subject distance. There's a lot more to know about flash photography with automatic and adjustable cameras. See pages 150–159 for more information.

Using Flash

The most important guide for successful flash photography is to keep within the flash range. For snapshot cameras, the range might be 4 to 12 feet. With more advanced flash, the range may vary. Check the instruction manual for your camera and flash.

Direct flash

light, but it may be rather harsh. Bounce the flash off a light, neutral-color wall, ceiling, or white card for a softer light more suitable for portraiture. Flash exposure depends on flash-to-subject distance. For more information on flash exposure and bounce flash, refer to pages 152–157.

...ced flash

Bounce Flash

Bouncing the flash off a ceiling or wall softens the harsh effect common to direct flash. It's easy with most cameras that accept accessory electronic flash units.

Some sensor-automatic electronic flash units will function automatically when you tilt the flash head toward the bounce surface. The sensor must remain aimed at your subject. Use the automatic mode that requires the largest lens aperture (smallest number), and stay well within the maximum flash range. Automatic units that have fixed heads must be used manually, as described below.

With a manual electronic flash unit or with one that has a fixed (non-tilting) flash head, you must remove the flash from the camera. You'll be able to connect flash and camera with a special electrical cord (PC-cord), sold by photo dealers. Make settings as follows. Determine the approximate distance that the flash will travel from flash to bounce surface to subject and use that distance to find the corresponding lens aperture on the flash calculator. Increase the recommended lens aperture by 2 f-stops and you have a good starting point for successful bounce flash exposure.

An effective bounce surface should be light-toned and neutral colored to reflect as much light as possible and to give natural color appearance. Make sure to aim the flash at a point midway between you and the subject so that the lighting will be even.

CANDID PICTURES

The word candid applies to family holiday celebrations as well as to stalking an interesting character on your travels. Your challenge is to photograph people in a natural atmosphere without calling attention to yourself. The reward is capturing the genuine emotions and expressions that give real clues to character.

There are two approaches to candid photography. One is to immerse yourself in whatever is going on, wait until the participants lose interest in you and resume their activity, and then start taking pictures. You can get totally natural, unselfconscious expressions—real slice-of-life material.

The other way is to find an unobtrusive position where you can remain unnoticed and take your pictures from a distance. Unless you use a camera that accepts auxiliary telephoto lenses, your subjects may appear a bit too distant. A normal or wide-angle lens such as that found on most snapshot or automatic cameras, actually helps you get good results when you're in the middle of the action as described above.

It may be helpful to preset your focus and use a small aperture, a fast shutter speed, and a fast film. This way you can concentrate on your subjects rather than divert attention to your adjustments.

CHILDREN

Children resemble adults in many ways, except that they're smaller and faster. Because they're smaller you must move closer to get a full-sized image in your picture. You'll also have to get down for an eye-level view. Children behave more naturally when the photographer is on their level.

Because they're so fast, you'll want to take the following precautions. Use a fast shutter speed—1/250 second or faster, if possible. Use flash indoors to capture the movement. Don't ask for poses or antics until you're completely ready to shoot. Use a high-speed film that will allow you a small aperture for maximum depth of field. (See page 142 for more information about depth of field.) The greater the range in acceptably sharp focus, the better chance you'll have to get sharp pictures of a quick youngster. Needless to say, if you have a game or some activity prearranged in a certain location, you should have all the time you need to take fine pictures while the child is occupied.

Most children have soft, clear skin that doesn't improve with harsh shadows. Backlighting, shady spots, and overcast days will portray any child's smooth complexion.

Above
A child's discovery can provide memorable pictures. Make sure to move close. Get down for a better view of the activity and the expressions. Be ready for one or more special moments.

Right
The soft light from a shaded window gently illuminates the subtle tones of a child's skin. Because such a scene is fairly dim, consider a high-speed film for sharp pictures.

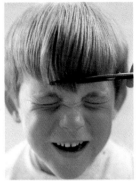

ELDERLY

A flattering portrait calls for soft, even lighting that will play down wrinkles and/or other complexion irregularities. Such a portrait might be made outdoors in the shade or on an overcast day or indoors with indirect light from outside. Bounce flash provides another possibility. Your subject will be more relaxed and comfortable if involved in one of his or her typical activities, and you'll get more natural expressions. Remember, keep the picture simple by avoiding or removing objects that will clutter or distract.

On the other hand, if you want to emphasize character displayed in a weather-beaten face or in gnarled hands, you will want strong directional lighting to give shape to the lines and to enhance the texture. Sidelighting can be very effective for this, and it needn't be terribly harsh. Too strong a light will cause so much contrast that you'll lose the fine gradations between highlight and shadow.

WEDDINGS

The volume of emotion at a wedding is usually far greater than at any other occasion. To the amateur photographer this is doubly important. First, you'll see more potential pictures than you can probably take. Second, the pictures you do take can have a rich significance in the years to come.

Since everyone wants to have a good time, including the photographer, try to plan ahead. Figure out what activities you want to record and ask the bride for a timetable and a list of locations. Check to see if you can take pictures in the church—particularly if you plan to use flash. If you feel strongly about planning, visit the locations beforehand to choose picture-taking spots and to choose what films you'll want (if there's a possibility of taking existing-light photos).

The next important step is to anticipate possible activity spots before a crowd gathers. This way

Getting ready.

you'll have the best vantage points. Take plenty of pictures. If you think you missed the most dramatic moment of the cake cutting, for instance, persuade the couple to do it again. Incidentally, let the professional photographer cover the wedding without interference. Professionals are fast and decisive and usually will allow you plenty of opportunity to get great shots.

One advantage you'll have is knowing some of the family and guests. Watch the live wires of the crowd for delightful candid snapshots. These informal pictures you'll take of people and happenings between the main events will be treasured by all concerned, particularly the bride and groom. In fact, you can give a very nice after-wedding present, if you make up a small album of your best shots. Everyone remembers weddings through pictures—the more the merrier.

People at weddings are usually paying attention to the proceedings. You get great opportunities to capture friends and relatives being themselves. If you have a loaded camera, ready for action, you should get a wonderful collection of memories.

PLACES

Landscapes closely follow people in popularity with most photographers. The reasons are as varied as the pictures, but several stand out—landscapes are beautiful and interesting; they provoke the imagination, and they provide a photographic challenge. Transferring the appearance and emotion of the scene from the mind to the film has been a lifetime quest for some photographers.

How often do photographers revel in the panorama stretched before them only to sigh with disappointment when they view their pictures? Although there are a number of hints that we'll discuss for better scenic shots, the most important advice we can give is: analyze *why* you're struck by a particular view and try to transfer your feelings to camera techniques. Ask these questions:

1. What elements of the scene interest you most? Trees, mountains, water, etc?

2. Do you want mostly sky, land, or water?

3. Is the scene more interesting as a horizontal or as a vertical?

4. Are colors or shapes more important?

Only you can answer these questions, of course, because you are the one who will be looking at the scene. The next few pages will offer some tools to help you get the answers into your pictures.

Pictures are reminders. As time passes, the memories get dimmer and dimmer. Moods and feelings are particularly difficult to recapture. Pictures help keep those memories bright—memories of the places you've seen and the wonders that leave you breathless. It's important to consider some of the ways to capture the sensations you feel in a particular place. Lighting and camera position are especially important. Notice in the picture at right how the slanting shadows of early morning help to define the shapes and bulk of the seaside cliffs? See also the subtle impression of distance offered by the haze in the scene. These ideas and others will be discussed in this chapter.

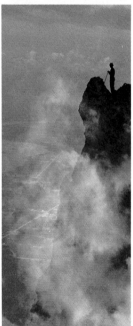

Question 1. Whatever part of the scene interests you the most, concentrate on it. No matter how vast the sight, you need one important center of interest. Otherwise the picture will lack impact. Making your camera respond generally means moving closer (making the subject bigger) and possibly shifting angles to eliminate anything extra and unwanted.

Question 2. If the sky is an important element in the picture, aim the camera to capture more sky, less land. If the sky only provides a horizon, aim the camera down for less sky.

Question 3. If the scene is broad and magnificent, such as a mountain-range horizon, hold the camera horizontally. If the scene seems to stretch from your toes into the distance—a river or a highway—for instance—then hold the camera vertically.

Horizontal

Vertical

74

Question 4. Sometimes dark shapes and light shapes interact in a way that catches your eye. Find a position and aim your camera so that you concentrate on those shapes only. Anything else in the picture only serves to dilute the image. At other times you'll see colors interplay in a provocative way. Again, choose a location and aim your camera so that the areas of color dominate the picture.

Dark and light shapes.

75

Composition

Good composition means placing the elements of a picture in a harmonious, interesting, and even unusual way to capture attention. In setting up a composition, consider the following:

Rule of thirds

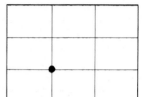

Balance Do you want a symmetrical arrangement or a casual collection? A symmetrical design has obvious balance. But even an informal composition is balanced so that it feels complete and stable. Colors, shadows, and light areas tend to balance each other, and are affected by big shapes, little shapes, distance, and lines.

Rule of Thirds A traditional way that artists have grouped elements in pictures is called the rule of thirds. Place the center of interest and important subordinate elements near intersections of vertical and horizontal lines at 1/3 points of the picture.

Framing

Scale

Perspective How do you make a two-dimensional picture express the depth and vastness of a three-dimensional scene? Carefully. Here are ideas.

Framing means almost surrounding your distant subject with some nearby foreground material, such as overhanging branches. The contrast between the near objects and the distant subject can help to establish distance. Framing is also helpful for disguising a dull, boring sky or hiding unwanted scene elements.

Similar to framing is the general use of objects in the foreground as subjects for scale to measure the background. Almost anything can be effective: a car, cactus, boulder, relative, motorcycle, boat (on water, of course), cabin, and more. The size of your scale subject will help give an impression of distance. If too close, viewers will forget the scene. At a medium distance the comparison may be most striking; at a greater distance the reference presents a more subtle view, but the viewer who stops for a second glance may be awed by how the landscape swallows up the extra subject.

77

Planes (orange filter)

Lines

Planes Some stunning views, particularly from high up in the mountains and desert, show subjects at different distances. Parallel mountain ranges (running across your field of vision) become hazy as they become more distant. This phenomenon is called aerial perspective. It is particularly obvious in the photo above, taken in Brazil at an early-morning hour when mist still shrouded the cone-like peaks. In the desert, beige sand turns foggy blue near the horizon. Use these separate planes of different color to help establish distance and scale.

Lines Lines that lead far into the scene can also help establish distance. A fence, a row of telephone poles, a road, or a river, all shrink as they recede from the camera, and this will be captured on film. Lines can also help to draw near and distant areas together into a harmonious picture. The cultivated rows in the picture at left provide continuous threads that link foreground and background into a single, tranquil scene.

Frontlighting

Backlighting

LIGHTING

Lighting Angles If you recall the discussion of lighting angles in the "People" section (page 49), you'll remember frontlighting, sidelighting, and backlighting. Although generalizing is always dangerous, sidelighting may be the most effective landscape lighting. Perhaps it's wise to broaden sidelighting to include any angle that does not produce direct front- or backlighting.

You need shadows to help show distance. Frontlighting gives no shadows. Backlighting can give dramatic shadows, but your subject may become a silhouette. Sidelighting from a wide series of angles casts shadows that help you gain an illusion of perspective. Waiting for the right times of day or carefully choosing your position may be the best answers.

Sidelighting

Time and Light As you've noticed, the landscape changes appearance dramatically from dawn to dusk and throughout the seasons. Obviously, seasonal changes mean green leaves, red leaves, or no leaves, as well as snow or soft grass. But the subtle changes come with changes in the light. Winter light is harsh but weak; summer light is rich but often oppressive. Sunlight in fall and spring is bright and cheerful. At noon the sun's rays beat straight down, flattening form and perspective. Early in the morning and late afternoon the light is a rich, warm color and long shadows streak across the scene.

Although you can't always choose the season, especially when traveling, you can often select the best time of day to make your landscape photographs. Early morning may be misty with light of a delicate rose color. Shadows are soft and violet, and the distance may be smoky. At noon the smaller shadows are hard and dense. Distance may be difficult to show. In the late afternoon, the light becomes more orange and the large shadows are warm and rich. The distance may be clear but will contrast in blue against the warmer foreground.

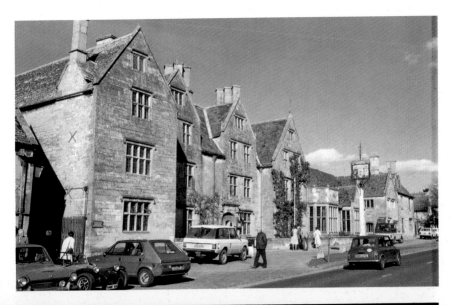

TRAVEL

Many people take most of their year's pictures during vacation or travel times. They see new sights and enjoy exciting experiences—experiences they want to deposit in their memory banks and share with others.

Travel photography combines all the elements discussed in this book—people, landscapes, interesting objects, flowers, night scenes, and sports. The challenge is being ready for all at the same time. Here are some general ideas, followed by specific tips that should make your travel photography easier.

Research As you plan the details of your trip, list important sights that you'll want to photograph. Then you'll have a ready reference to assist your memory. Of course, you'll find special places of interest not listed in any guide book. Many of these will give your pictures a more authentic local flavor than the customary landmarks—the early morning marketplace, people involved in unique craft work, unusual methods of transportation, and, of course, the preparation of those special meals.

Early morning shadows and foreground branches create perspective in this gorgeous view of Neuschwanstein Castle near Füssen, Germany.

Right
Pictures of people add character to your travel memories. Ask permission and get a winning expression from a classical dancer in Cochin, India.

82

Take Plenty of Pictures Once back home, the typical sentiment is, "Why didn't we take more?" Film is a small part of your travel budget, but the pictures will be a large part of later enjoyment.

Look for the best angles and positions from which to photograph your subjects. Sometimes you'll find that you can improve the composition of your first picture by shifting your position.

When photographing colorful, fast-moving events, keep looking through the viewfinder. Take pictures as often as you see something you like.

Many Subjects Be prepared to move in close, with permission of course, to people in native or ethnic dress. Photograph camel caravans, shop windows full of curios, floral displays, festivals, parades, local sports, children, building interiors, and illuminated sights at night. Remember that many of your best-treasured pictures will be of the subjects you found unique—the ones that you reacted to most strongly. Also, don't worry about bad weather. Fine photos can come from inclement conditions— umbrellas in the rain, fishing boats at anchor in the fog, and children playing in the snow.

Be Prepared Keep your camera with you at all times, ready and loaded, and be alert for good picture situations.

Tell a Story Your travel pictures should describe the vacation as completely as possible. Don't forget to capture events that will help you remember. Airplane flights, train trips, taxi rides, customs officials, hotels, tourguides—all these contribute to the later enjoyment of your vacation. Many travelers photograph signs as memory joggers. Signs are even better when familiar faces surround them.

Personalize Your Pictures Have family or tour group members pose in pictures of monuments, scenic views, restaurants, and with the helpful local people you'll meet. You'll delight in the warmer significance of these scenes later.

Tips Here are some specifics that might help.

1. Before you leave home, look at your list of possible pictures, and pack about twice as much film as you think you'll need.

2. Allow enough time to take a roll of film with your camera and have it processed before you leave. It's a good way to make sure that your camera is operating correctly.

3. During travel preparation, register all foreign-made photo equipment with U.S. customs, so that misunderstandings about duty won't arise on your return. Most Federal office buildings include a Custom House office where an official will inventory your equipment and give you the proper document to surrender to customs officials when you return. Sales receipts may be enough documentation.

4. Don't forget flash pictures. Take whatever batteries, flash devices, or current transformers you'll need.

5. When passing through airport security, ask for hand-inspection of your camera and all film, exposed and unexposed. It's not always possible. Security x-rays can be harmful to your film—the more x-rays the worse the harm. Anytime you avoid the x-ray scanners will help the final results.

6. For extra convenience in the U.S., take film processing mailers with you. Send the exposed film back in the mail to minimize exposure to x-rays. Your processed pictures should be waiting for you when you return.

7. It is a sensible practice to examine your camera at night after touring is finished for the day. Clean the lens if necessary, and check the battery if your camera uses one. Make sure that the carrying strap is secure.

8. Keep your camera with you—to avoid theft and to keep ready for picture opportunities. An unattended camera can be an inviting prize.

PETS

Pets have as much personality as people, and pictures should communicate those traits. You'll need some ingenuity, lots of patience, and a good location. Small animals, of course, can be photographed nearly anywhere. Larger pets will give you less choice. Above all, find a setting that appears natural.

Animals, like children, have limited patience and a short attention span. Set up your camera and

Horses might be best in a field.

A working dog might be best in a field, a house cat on a window sill or in front of the fire. Try to keep the background simple.

Flash is an effective way to separate a small animal from confusing surroundings indoors. Flash can also stop quick movement. Move in close enough to eliminate other elements in the picture.

Make sure that you stay in the minimum focus range of the camera. Also, see that you are still within the flash range of your camera. If you are still in focus, but too close for the flash, put one or two layers of white tissue over the flash to cut down the light. When you're all set to take a flash picture, try to spark an interesting expression.

get completely ready to take pictures before you bring your subject on stage.

Ingenuity means keeping your pet in the same place and evoking appealing, enthusiastic expressions. Find or devise a noisemaker that will prick up your pet's ears for an alert look. Getting a pet to stay may call for a morsel of favorite food.

Be patient. When you see what you want, take plenty of pictures. Pets soon grow restless.

Get fairly close—enough so that your subject fills the viewfinder. Place the camera down at the pet's eye level, just as you would for a small child. The perspective gives a less distorted view, and animals appreciate the eye-level approach.

Some animals have special photogenic habits. Famous animal photographer Walter Chandoha made one of his first commercially successful pet photos of his cat Minguina, who made a long stretch in front of a mirror after every nap. Chandoha got ready and snapped her in the middle of the stretch—just what an eager art director wanted for an advertisement.

Most pets can move pretty fast when inspired. Practice the stunt you want to capture with an unloaded camera. When everything looks right, start taking pictures.

89

ZOOS

Everybody likes the zoo, and your zoo photos should show it. You can take pictures of the animals and pictures of people enjoying the animals. For best results in photographing the animals themselves, get as close as safely possible. Dangerous inhabitants are usually behind bars, wire, or glass. From behind the barriers in a safe position, aim your camera through the wire or between the bars or put it right next to the glass. Make sure to stay behind zoo-imposed barriers. Wild animals are always unpredictable. There's no sense offering yourself as a free meal if the city has already provided one.

Where there are fewer restrictions, it's easier to get unobstructed photos. As always, see if you can find a position with superior lighting and background. Move around until you find the best.

The petting zoo is often one of the most fertile areas for great spontaneous pictures—especially with your kids. Most youngsters are thrilled and awed by all the furry, friendly creatures, and their faces show it. Move in close enough to capture those rapturous expressions.

Some zoos have indoor displays where you can take flash pictures (pages 150–159) or existing-light pictures (see page 163) of the exhibits. Put camera and flash next to the glass where possible. Where you're separated from the glass, take your pictures at an angle so that flash reflections won't bounce back at your camera.

You can get fantastic results at the attractions where spectators are caged in autos and the inhabitants roam free. The wild animals are familiar with autos and will venture quite close. Use extreme caution, however, and carefully obey the rules. A charging carnivore has more primitive things in mind than portrait photography. If you're in a car with the windows down, just stay inside the window. If the windows are closed and the car is moving, hold the camera next to but not touching the glass. You'll avoid reflections and get sharper pictures. Use as fast a shutter speed as possible to overcome car or animal movement.

Surprisingly, time of day may be important for zoo pictures. At peak visitation periods during the weekend, the animals may retire to their hideaways just to avoid the crowds. Midday is usually a time for napping in the animal kingdom. Try to schedule a special trip with friends or family to see the creatures when they're likely to be most active—during the week, preferably in the morning before feeding time.

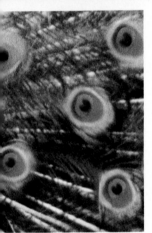

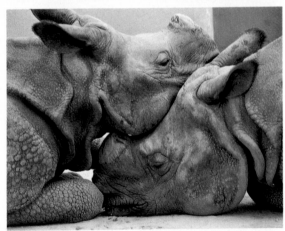

FLOWERS AND PLANTS

Any flower garden is a cornucopia of nature's greatest treasures—dazzling colors and soft fragrances combined in a master patchwork of cosmic design. Some "gardens" are wild, growing free, while others are carefully planned and cultivated. In either case, there are some simple techniques that should give you exciting pictures.

Concentrate on the garden—move in close enough to picture only the blooms. Better yet, take pictures at different distances to show the overall view and then smaller segments of floral glory. Get very close with close-up lenses. (See page 182.) Move around so that you have the best background and picture design. Take pictures when the light makes nature's work most attractive. The best times are early in the morning with soft shadows and sparkling dew or the rich warm light of late afternoon.

Take pictures throughout the growing season so that you have a complete record to share with distant friends or relatives.

Look for exciting pictures of nature subjects in all the seasons. Fall leaves, snow-covered pine needles, and the first crocuses give extra dimension to the year's picture-taking.

Close-Up Tips A piece of colored construction paper will provide a simple background that concentrates attention on your subject. Flash or a piece of white cardboard will reflect light into shadow areas. Since you'll be very close, cover a flash with two or more layers of tissue for correct exposure. If the breeze is batting your subject around, make a quick windbreak of tomato stakes and sheet plastic. For that extra-fresh look, create some artificial dew with an atomizer.

BUILDINGS

What's important about a particular building? Or, rather, why do you like a special building? What are the features that attract you? Once you've isolated these aspects, concentrate on them.

In the illustration above, the photographer sensed peace and stability in the weatherbeaten harbor structures. This feeling is augmented by the nearly perfect reflection. Although cropped for best

94

page design, the breadth of the long, low buildings is captured by horizontal framing. The misty surroundings create a mood of New England nostalgia which seems to await the arrival of a transatlantic square-rigger. Another case might show a martial row of brilliantly gingerbreaded row houses. Naturally, you'll want to capture the pattern of the row, as well as individual details.

Details might be ornate or stately entrances, wrought-iron work, or designs in the brick or stonework of the facade. Again, wait for a time of day when the light shows off your subject, and move in close to isolate what you want to capture.

COLLECTIBLES AND OBJETS D'ART

Many hobbyists make or collect things that they want to show other like-minded people. They also see things on display that they want to record. Same important rules—move in close (with a close-up lens, if necessary. See page 182). Find a camera position that sees a simple background, and use lighting that shows off the object's best features. If necessary, use reflectors to fill in shadows. One good way to control your results is to cover a table with plain cloth or paper, preferably not white, that contrasts with your subject. Raise the cloth or paper up out of sight in the background to provide an undistracting backdrop. Outdoors in sunlight you can control the lighting by turning the table. Indoors with photolamps (see page 56), you can move the lights.

The free-form ceramic statuettes pictured at left were photographed in the set-up shown above. Indirect window light provided the main illumination, while a white reflector card filled the dark-side shadows.

ACTION

There are some familiar ideas for capturing action successfully as well as several specific techniques. Following a few general tips are ideas about portraying movement.

Get as close as you safely can. Choose a position that will dramatize the incident. Look for an uncluttered background and good lighting. Preset your camera controls and focus on the spot where you plan to capture your subject. When the moving body arrives at the spot, snap the picture. When composing the picture, leave a little room in front of your subject—it looks more natural.

STOPPING THE ACTION

You can usually freeze movement sharply in one of four ways. You can set a fast shutter speed on your camera (see pages 136-139). The faster the shutter speed, the more likely your chances of a sharp moving subject. Camera position will help, too. You can also catch some movement at its peak, or you can pan your camera with the subject.

Peak of Action Some motions have a midpoint where everything stops momentarily. A diver at the top of an upward spring or a basketball player up for a dunk both stop before descending. A baseball pitcher or hitter, a tennis player, a golfer all pause before moving and stop after follow-through. Practice for a while without film. Follow a diver to the mid-air pause and pretend you're snapping that fraction of a second. Get a golfing friend to practice swings. See if you can capture the stationary highpoint of both backswing and follow-through.

Panning Panning works with running kids, dogs, horses, bicycles, race cars, speed boats, or airplanes during take off. You may have to pan for two reasons. First, the subject may be moving so fast that even a fast shutter speed cannot stop the action. Second, good composition is difficult because the subject is in your viewfinder for such a short time. Swing both your camera and body so that the moving subject stays in the same place in your viewfinder. This, too, takes practice. Rotate your body smoothly and concentrate on pressing the shutter release at the best point for picture design. Follow through after you snap the shutter. Unless you can choose a very fast shutter speed, chances are good that the subject will be sharp and the background will be blurred into attractive streaks of color.

Toward the camera

Direction The direction of movement may affect your choice of technique. A subject coming toward or retreating from you is easier to capture sharp than one crossing your field of vision. You can use a slower shutter speed for action toward or away from you, and you'll find that you have more time to make a good composition. Subjects moving at a 90° angle to you and your camera invite panning and your fastest shutter speeds.

1/500 second at 90°

1/30 second at 90°

BLURRED ACTION

Blurred motion can convey the idea of speed and movement. Set a very slow shutter speed (1/30 to 1/8 second) on your camera. You can pan or hold the camera steady while the subject's blurred movements cover a little bigger slice of time on your film. When the camera is mounted on a tripod or other solid support, only the subject will be blurred. Add your own movement by handholding the camera.

SPORTS TIPS

Get close to the players. Ask permission for a sideline spot at amateur and school competition. At professional events choose an unobstructed position as near the action as possible.

Prefocus on the spot where you'll get the best picture. Have your camera loaded and the exposure controls set. It's very helpful to know the game, because you can anticipate key plays and key players. Photograph night games and indoor events by the existing light. See pages 160-163.

NIGHT

The world spends half its time in light and half in darkness. Picture-taking at night can be just as exciting as daytime photography.

You'll find subjects everywhere—bright lights, fireworks, holiday displays, and outdoor activities. Snapshot camera owners can use flash outdoors at night. A high-speed film will extend the flash range. Owners of automatic or adjustable cameras can take pictures with flash or with the existing light. High-speed films, slow shutter speeds, and a large maximum aperture will help capture almost anything that can be seen. See pages 160-163 for more existing-light recommendations.

BAD WEATHER

Everybody takes pictures when the sun is out. But on some days, it rains, snows, mists, or is just plain overcast. The truth is that some of your best pictures can happen on days with poor weather. Think of the benefits.

People look their best out of the sun. Their faces open up with bright, natural, unshadowed expressions. Light overcast days are perfect for outstanding portraits. Just make sure that your background doesn't include much dull sky and move in close to your subject. You may even find that rain and snow give people, kids especially, an opportunity to wear colorful clothing and engage in activities you'll want to capture. In rain or snow, take care to protect your camera. Keep it warm and dry under a slicker or parka.

Scenery takes on a very different appearance on a dull day. Although the sky appears gloomy and grim, the colors of grass and trees, red barns, and white fences can appear brighter. Fog will lend an ethereal quality to many scenes—subjects may appear partly shrouded in mist. Subjects may appear bluish in pictures made while the sun is hiding. Attach an 81A filter* to your camera lens to warm up the colors a bit. You won't need to change your exposure.

Snow and cold give a soft, blurry appearance in pastel shades. With your camera protected from flakes and the cold, you'll find a world full of children, sleds, snowmen, skiers, and colorful outerwear. At night, you can take unusual flash pictures of nearby subjects with snowflakes hovering all around.

Rain brings some charming surprises. Bright umbrellas and colorful rain gear, for instance. Reflections in puddles or on rain-drenched streets give another dimension to your pictures. Keep your camera out of the water, but don't hesitate to shoot activity in a rainshower. Find a good position to snap the action from under an overhang, or inside a car with the window open.

*See pages 168-169 for more on filters.

Overcast skies give delightful casual portraits, because your subjects won't be squinting into the sun. Try not to include much of the dull sky, and you'll find bright, colorful subjects all around. Again, high-speed film will help you get well-exposed pictures with a snapshot camera. Remember that your family and other people don't suspend activity when the sun goes under. Sometimes a gloomy day will inspire children to try something new. If they don't think of anything, suggest an interesting activity that will get them occupied and yield good pictures.

Mist or fog can lend a ghostly, ethereal appearance to familiar scenes. Nearby subjects will be distinct, but more distant subjects will seem to be

fading into another dimension. Often, there's bright light coming through the mist, spotlighting bright objects or making trails through the heavy air. Early morning is a perfect time to search out misty scenes. If the sky is dark overhead, use a high-speed film in a snapshot camera.

EXPOSURE
Bad weather is darker, and you'll need more exposure than in sunlight. See pages 130-139 for film choice and exposure setting information. Automatic cameras, of course, will adjust to scene lighting with very little help from you. Use high-speed film in a snapshot camera.

109

SHOWING YOUR PICTURES

Good pictures are meant to be seen. Here are some ideas for getting more mileage from your best efforts. (Make sure you read page 113 for information about storing and protecting your photos.)

PHOTO ALBUMS

Albums abound in shapes and sizes from a purse-size book to coffee-table volumes. You can also make your own with a loose-leaf binder, thin cardboard pages, and photo cement or white glue. Many people assemble their albums chronologically—it seems sensible. They also label the pictures *and* the negative-envelopes so that they can get reprints at a much later date.

Some people get more in albums by cutting up the prints and inserting the best parts. There's wasted space in almost every print.

A photo album can be the chronicle of years or an up-to-date newsbrief filled with your latest snapshots.

ENLARGEMENTS AND HOME DÉCOR

Another way to get your best images out of the box and into view is to display enlargements. Available from your photofinisher in different sizes (5x7, 8x10, 11x14, and 16x20 inches) and shapes to fit your film format, enlargements are ideal for framing or for gifts. Hung on a wall, displayed on a desk, or even commanding an important place in your albums, enlargements have a powerful ability to cross the barriers of time and say, "You were there." For more ideas on decorating with photographs, see the KODAK Photo Book *Photo Décor,* available from your photo dealer.

Traditional and unusual ways of displaying prints are available from your local photo, stationery, department, or discount store. You'll see frames in dozens of styles as well as such different ideas as photo cubes, wall clocks, mobiles, and collage boards.

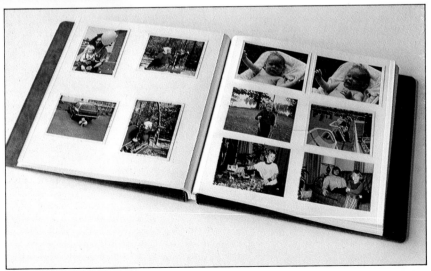

GREETING CARDS

A card with a picture of you or you and your family is truly a personal communication. Children grow, houses change, and so do the seasons. You can commission special greetings from your photofinisher with pictures and words all printed together, or you can attach a print to the inside of other cards. You can send 3 1/2 x 5-inch prints as postcards. Make sure you use a pen that will write on the slick, plastic back of the print. Some people plan ahead and have favorite shots reprinted to enclose in letters to distant friends and relatives. A photo Christmas card each year keeps the people on your mailing list in closer touch with a growing family.

PROCESSING SERVICES

In addition to reprints, enlargements, and photo-greeting cards, your photofinisher can make slides from negatives, prints and enlargements made from slides, and copyprints from other prints. Some photofinishers can help you crop the negatives you want enlarged to improve the picture design.

Greeting cards for many occasions are available from your photofinisher. Can you guess which holiday cards receive the most attention?

STORING PICTURES

With a little care and forethought, your pictures will provide you with many years of pleasure. Here are some general ideas for prolonging the lives of prints, slides, and negatives.

Storage Locations You want a place with moderate temperature (under 70° F [21°C]) and fairly low humidity (under 50% relative humidity) which probably eliminates most basements and attics. Heat can become excessive in an attic, and humidity in either place may be harmful. A spot near a chimney, heat run, or in direct window light can cause problems as well.

Containers An album is the best way to display and protect your prints. Since the prints will be in intimate contact with the pages, make sure that the materials used in the construction of the album will not harm the prints. Check with your photo dealer about the cover, pages, plastic sleeves, mounting corners or hinges, and the ink used for identification. This becomes especially important if you have prints without the negatives. If you have the negatives, you can have them reprinted.

Album prints should not be subjected to pressure, nor should the image sides of the prints be in direct contact with each other. Protect the faces of the prints in an album with a suitable plastic sheeting.

If you're making your own album, be sure that the adhesive you use for adhering the prints is photographically safe. Starch paste, animal glue, and rubber cement are not advised. One of the safest methods is mounting prints on album pages with special dry-mounting tissue. Ask your photo dealer for specific recommendations.

You'll want to find a safe home for negatives and extra prints. The envelopes provided by most photofinishers are suitable for storing prints and negatives because they contain no contaminants that would ruin the images. Other containers may have ingredients that will quickly harm photos. The same applies to furniture drawers, attics, and basements where fumes from mothballs, cosmetics, chemicals, glues, or wood-finishing products can cause damaging chemical reactions.

Don't store prints and negatives under pressure—they may stick together. In fact, if you have real favorites, they should be separated into plastic photo sleeves for safekeeping.

SLIDE SHOWS

Most people who take slides like to see that big bright image up on the screen. Because it's so big, it can be shared with many people at the same time, and modern projection equipment can show many slides in a comparatively short time. On the other hand, everyone nods in sympathy when a friend mentions that three of last evening's hours were devoted to someone's slide show or home movies. With a little planning and restraint, you can have your audiences clamoring for more.

First, arrange your slides so that they tell a story, even if it's a simple chronological story of vacation travel. You'll find that narration is easier when you can proceed logically from one topic to the next. Second, use only your best slides. Pass over pictures that are fuzzy or incorrectly exposed. Resist the temptation to show everything. Third, don't leave any one slide on the screen too long—10 seconds is a

Selecting pictures
Choose only your best pictures— ones that are sharp and correctly exposed. Poor-quality pictures are tiring to view and lower the impact of your show. One easy way to look at slides is with the help of an inexpensive illuminator, available from most photo dealers. Project your final choices to check their sharpness.

useful average time. If you have to spend a long time explaining a picture, chances are that it's not a very good illustration. Your audience is used to TV and movies where things generally happen pretty fast. Fourth, consider one hour the maximum time that people can sit still comfortably. Fifth, rehearse your presentation a few times, so that you're familiar with the order of the slides and so that your narration will flow easily. Sixth, get everything— screen, projector, and chairs—set up in advance. And make sure that you have a spare projector bulb and know how to change it.

These are easy preplanning steps, but you may be surprised at the enthusiasm of your audience. If you think you want to delve deeper into slide presentations, consult Keith Boas' article in *The Ninth Here's How*—a KODAK Photo Book available from most photo dealers.

Telling a Story
The easiest way to tell a story with pictures is to put them in chronological order. Since every story has certain key elements or events, use the pictures that best portray the highpoints. You don't have to explain or show every step. Just include the necessary pictures. Too many will dilute the message.

1. Getting ready.

2. Frosting the cake.

3. Making the presentation.

PHOTO REPORTS

There are times when photos are more striking than words alone. Reports for business, school, and even your community are more effective when amplified by pictures. You can create a slide show or illustrate a written report with captioned prints, or consider enlargement displays in public places. Here's what's important. The pictures should clearly show exactly what you want them to show. Use no more than you need—too many dilute impact. Make sure that the technical quality is good—sharp and well-exposed pictures. Captions or narration should be short and to the point.

PHOTO INVENTORY

Nobody likes to face the idea of calamity, but that's why insurance companies exist. In case of a loss, it's helpful to provide as much evidence as possible. Pictures can be a valuable resource.

Take a moment to make a mental inventory of your possessions and how much it would cost to replace them. With this incentive, you might want to load and use your camera. A series of photographs can effectively document your goods, particularly when combined with the sales receipts.

Start with your home—the outside and the inside. Take pictures outside when the scene is bright and when important features aren't hidden in shadow. Shoot from all important viewpoints, and maybe a few more for extra precaution. When inside, take pictures of the four walls in each room with flash or existing light. (Don't forget to include some of the floor with costly rugs or carpet.)

Once you have covered all the exterior and interior features of the house, begin recording from a closer distance the smaller items such as silver flatware, fine china, paintings, objets d'art, clothes, tools, small appliances, sports equipment, antique furniture, and jewelry. The same applies to lawn and garden equipment, outside furniture, and so on.

Keep the prints and negatives or slides in your safe deposit box in case you ever need them to prove a loss.

HAS IT HAPPENED TO YOU?

Sometimes things go wrong, and you get results you didn't plan *or* want. Here are some of the most common problems, the reasons, and some suggested solutions.

Camera movement

Problem	Reason	Solution
Fuzzy, unsharp pictures	Shutter speed too slow.	For pictures of still subjects, use a shutter speed no slower than 1/30 second if handholding the camera. For fast-moving subjects, use the fastest shutter speed possible—usually no slower than 1/250 second. (See page 139.)
	Incorrect handling.	Make sure you hold the camera very steady and gently press the shutter release. (See page 42.)
	Incorrect focus.	Make sure you focus correctly on your subject. Refer to your camera manual. (See page 43.)
	Dirty lens.	Keep your lens clean of dust and smears. (See page 186.)

Out of focus

Dirty lens

Problem	Reason	Solution
Pictures too light, too dark	Incorrect film speed setting on camera or on handheld meter.	Set or check the film speed every time you load a new roll of film. (See page 34.)
	Dead or weak meter battery.	Check battery periodically according to camera instruction manual. Replace at least once a year.
	No adjustment for side- and back-lighting.	See page 140 for information about adjusting for different lighting angles.
Pictures occasionally too light	Shutter may be sticking.	See competent camera repair person.
Blank negatives (no prints) or black slides	Shutter does not open.	See camera repair person.
	Film does not advance through camera.	Check loading procedures in instruction manual or have repair person check film-advance mechanism.
	Lens cap not removed.	Make sure you remove lens cap.
Pictures consistently too light or dark	Exposure meter may need adjustment.	See repair person.

Too light

Correct exposure

Too dark

Problem	Reason	Solution
Flash pictures too light, dark	Light—too close to subject. Dark—too far from subject.	Check snapshot camera distance range or check focus setting with adjustable/automatic camera. (See page 150.)
	Film speed on camera/flash unit wrong.	Check to see that correct film speed is set on flash unit or camera. (See page 152.)
	Aperture setting wrong.	Make sure that aperture setting on camera agrees with information on flash calculator dial. (See pages 153-154.)
Flash too dark	Dark—electronic flash may not have fully recycled.	Allow flash to recycle fully until ready light shows or maybe a bit longer.
	Weak batteries.	(See page 155.) Change batteries.
People or animals with glowing eyes	Flash positioned too close to lens for subject with open retina.	Turn on all room lights. If possible, remove flash from camera to increase distance between lens and flash. Increase flash-to-subject distance. Have person avert eyes.

Too dark

Correctly exposed

Too light

Problem	Reason	Solution
Flash pictures: black slides, blank negatives, and no prints	Flash didn't fire.	Battery dead, poor connection between flash and camera. (See page 152.)
Glare spots in flash pictures	Flash fired into reflective background.	Adjust your position so that any reflective material (mirrors, paneled walls, eyeglasses) is at an angle.
Flash pictures unevenly exposed	Foreground object closer than main subject—gets overexposed.	Use a position where the main subject is closest to the flash.
Flash pictures partly exposed	Incorrect shutter speed.	Check your camera manual for correct shutter speed with flash. (See page 152.)

Foreground object

Object removed

Wrong shutter speed

Reflection from shiny surface

Position changed to avoid reflection

Problem	Reason	Solution
Pictures with dark obstructions	Finger in front of lens. Material inside camera.	Check camera-holding position to make sure hand or fingers don't obstruct lens. Carefully check inside camera for foreign matter obstruction.
	Camera strap or case in front of lens.	Check that lens is clear of strap and case before taking picture.
Pictures with unusual color	Bluish—tungsten film used in daylight.	Make sure that the film matches the lighting conditions. If not, add a filter. (See page 167.)
	Yellowish-red—daylight film used in tungsten light.	If using daylight film in tungsten light, consider a filter. (See page 166.)
	Mottled, streaked, maybe greenish or muddy—film outdated.	Make sure you use fresh film and get it processed promptly. Check packing material for expiration date. Do not leave film in extremely hot places.

Finger blocking lens

Tungsten film in daylight

Daylight film in tungsten light

Problem	Reason	Solution
Pictures overlapped	Too many pictures on roll.	Don't try to squeeze one more shot at the end of the roll.
	Film winding mechanism needs adjustment.	See a competent repair person.
Light streaks and spots on pictures	Direct rays of light strike lens.	Don't shoot directly into the sun or other bright light source.
Consistent streaks and spots	Fogging: light leak in camera.	Have camera checked by competent repair person.
	Camera back opened accidentally.	Never open the camera without checking to see if it has film inside.
	Film handled in direct sunlight.	Load and unload your camera in the shade or other subdued light.
	Sticking shutter.	Have camera checked by competent repair person.
	X-ray exposure.	Ask for hand inspection of camera and film at airport security. (See page 87.)

Overlapped pictures

Direct rays of light

Camera back opened

SIMPLIFYING THE TECHNICALITIE

The more you know about any skill or activity, the better the results. This section of *How to Take Good Pictures* is devoted to how photography works and how to extend your knowledge for even better pictures under a greater variety of conditions.

We'll approach our goal—good pictures—in two ways. First we'll take a tour of a typical 35 mm camera to see what functions all the controls perform. We'll look at film to see what makes it work for you. We'll tie film and camera together into a discussion of exposure that will help you get better results in many tricky situations.

Then, after discussing the sketchy fundamentals of how you can control camera and film, we'll talk about some individual techniques that you'll want to sample. Flash, filters, existing light, and more will show you the delight of creation, where *you* control *your* photography.

CAMERA CONTROLS

All cameras have controls. The simplest camera might have only one control—the shutter release which you press to take a picture.

More complicated cameras may have several controls. Earlier in the book, we gave a short discussion of 35 mm camera operation—enough to help you start. Now we'll take an imaginary automatic 35 mm camera that is fairly complex and describe the function of all the moving parts you need to know about. Your camera may have some or all of the features we'll describe. And very likely some of the devices will be in different positions from those shown here. Compare these diagrams to those in your camera instruction manual.

For greater clarity, we've even repeated some functions. For example, if your camera has a pop-up flash, you probably won't have a flash hot shoe or a flash-cord socket.

Top Front View
1. *film-advance lever*
2. *film-frame counter*
3. *shutter release*
4. *shutter-speed dial*
5. *flash hot shoe*
6. *rewind knob*
7. *pop-up flash*
8. *pop-up flash button*
9. *viewfinder window*
10. *lens*
11. *aperture ring and mode selector (automatic, manual, possibly flash)*
12. *focusing ring*
13. *film-speed selector dial*
14. *self-timer*
15. *flash-cord socket*

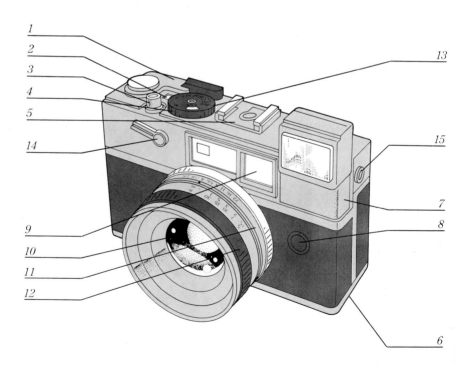

1. **Film-advance lever:** *By moving this lever one or more strokes after taking a picture, you advance the film to the next frame.*

2. **Film-frame counter:** *This shows you how many pictures you have taken: from loading steps to 12, 20, 24, or 36.*

3. **Shutter release:** *You press this button to take a picture.*

4. **Shutter-speed dial:** *This selects the shutter speed. It may include the film-speed selector or the automatic operation switch.*

5. **Flash hot shoe:** *This accepts an electronic flash unit. When you attach the flash, the electrical connection is complete.*

6. **Rewind knob:** *This knob usually has a fold-out lever to help rewind exposed film back into the magazine.*

7. **Pop-up flash:** *Raise and activate built-in flash with the button shown in callout 8. Turn off the flash by pressing down.*

8. **Pop-up flash button:** *This button raises and activates the built-in flash unit.*

9. **Viewfinder window:** *This is the other side of the window you look through to compose your picture.*

10. **Lens:** *The lens on your camera gathers and organizes light rays to make a sharp picture on your film.*

11. **Aperture ring:** *With this you select the lens aperture. The aperture ring may also control automatic, manual, or flash functions.*

12. **Focusing ring:** *You turn this to get sharp pictures of your subject. It may show distances as symbols or in feet and metres.*

Back View

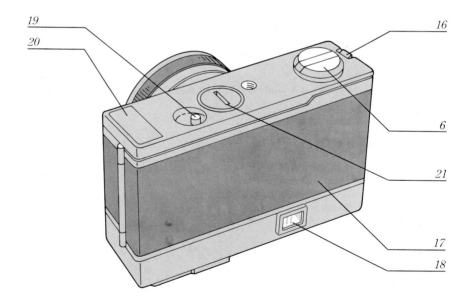

16. release for film-compartment door
17. film-compartment door

18. viewfinder window
19. film-advance release button

20. pop-up flash battery compartment
21. meter-battery compartment

13. **Film-speed selector dial:** *Every time you load film into your camera, set the film speed on the selector dial.*

14. **Self-timer:** *This device automatically snaps the shutter after it is triggered, which allows you to include yourself in the picture.*

15. **Flash cord socket:** *Plug the flash cord (PC cord) into this socket to complete the electrical connection between the flash and the camera.*

16. **Release for film-compartment door:** *After you rewind the exposed film, open the compartment door with this latch.*

17. **Film-compartment door:** *By operating the latch in callout 16, this door can be opened to load or unload film.*

18. **Viewfinder window:** *You look through this window to arrange your picture. You may also see focusing and exposure information.*

19. **Film-advance release button:** *This button releases the film-advance mechanism so that you can rewind the film.*

20. **Pop-up flash battery compartment:** *This compartment holds the batteries that supply the power to your built-in electronic flash.*

21. **Meter-battery:** *The battery for automatic or manual cameras with exposure meters should be changed at least once a year.*

129

FILM

Black-and-white negative   *Color negative*   *Color slide*

In addition to the film information on page 46 here is more information that will help you understand the next section on exposure.

SIZE
Film comes in different sizes and lengths: 110 for pocket-sized cameras, 126 for larger snapshot cameras, and 135 for 35 mm cameras. 110- and 126-size films generally give a choice of 12 or 24 exposures for color prints, 20 exposures for color slides. 135-size film offers several possibilities—12, 24, and 36 exposures for color prints and 20 and 36 exposures for color slides.

SLIDES OR PRINTS
Do you want slides to project or prints from negatives to pass around and put in albums? Slides projected on a screen are brilliant and beautiful, but slide film requires near-perfect exposure for good results. Prints are lovely, too, convenient to share, and negative film is somewhat tolerant of exposure error. You can have enlargements made from either.

Bright—slow or medium-speed film   *Dim—high-speed film*

SPEED

All films have a measured sensitivity to light, indicated by an assigned ISO, ASA, or DIN number. Slow- and medium-speed films—ISO/ASA 25, 32, 64, 100, 125—are intended for general picture-taking in daylight, while high-speed films—ISO/ASA 160, 200, and 400—are intended for low light. If you take pictures on dark days, indoors, or at night without flash, you'll want a high-speed film.

There are other considerations, too. Sharp pictures of action require fast shutter speeds (see the "Exposure" section, pages 136-139).

On the other hand, there's a good reason for choosing a slower, less sensitive film. With careful examination, prints or slides from high-speed films don't appear quite as sharp as those from the slower films. For scenic pictures you may decide that it's important to have as sharp an image as possible— from a film with a speed of ISO/ASA 25, perhaps.

Choosing a film speed is often a function of what's most important—extreme speed or extreme sharpness. If you don't need the extremes, stick to one of the medium-speed films, ISO/ASA 64 to ISO/ASA 125, which will be very sharp and still allow you enough speed for moderately fast action or a fairly wide range of lighting conditions.

COLOR BALANCE

Most films give natural-appearing colors in daylight or with flash. Some negative films respond almost as well to tungsten or fluorescent light. If you want correct color rendition in lighting other than daylight, choose a film balanced for a particular light source, or use color-correction filters. (See page 166 in the "Filters" section.)

Daylight—tungsten film   *Daylight—daylight film*

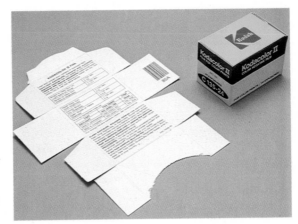

"When all else fails, read the instructions." Actually, the film data inside the box or on a sheet can be very helpful if your meter quits. Some of the information may even prove to be valuable casual reading.

FILM INSTRUCTIONS

Some of the handiest information around is in the instructions packaged with some films for automatic and adjustable cameras. You'll find data on exposure, flash, and filters. If your exposure meter quits, consult the instructions. If puzzled about filtration, see the inside of the box.

CARE

All film has a useful life. Usually there's an expiration date printed on the film box. Take pictures and have the film processed before that date.

Extremes in humidity and temperature are film's worst enemies. In heat and high humidity, protect your film and camera as well as you can. For instance, don't store them in the attic or basement. Don't leave them in direct sunlight, the glove compartment of your car, or a similar high-temperature environment. When taking pictures in cold dry air, keep your camera and film close to your body so that cold film won't get brittle and snap when it is advanced or rewound. Keeping your camera warm will also help prevent static electricity marks on your film.

Try to change film in the shade, even if it's the shade of your own body to help eliminate fog marks on your film from direct, bright sunlight.

EXPOSURE

Although automatic cameras successfully choose exposure settings without human help, understanding the rudiments of exposure can improve your picture-taking. There are four factors—scene brightness, film sensitivity, shutter speed, and aperture.

Extremely dim light. High-speed film (ISO/ASA 160-400) would be a must in this case.

SCENE BRIGHTNESS

Scene brightness can vary widely, from a sunny day at a beach with white sand to a somber plaza lighted only by a shaded street light. To record these extremes and all the variations in between, your photographic apparatus must be flexible.

FILM SENSITIVITY

As discussed on pages 131–132, film comes in a wide range of sensitivities, or speeds, for a wide range of lighting conditions and applications. Film speed helps determine camera exposure settings. Once you match the film to the situation, an ISO/ASA 100 film for fair weather for instance, then you or the camera must adjust the shutter speed and aperture.

Bright light. A slow- or medium-speed film (ISO/ASA 25-125) would work well here.

SHUTTER SPEED

The shutter speed controls the *length of time* that the shutter stays open. The longer the shutter is open, the more light it lets in. When open, it's usually for a very brief time, anywhere from 1/1000 second to 1/30 second. You can see the different speeds on your camera's shutter speed control: 1000 (1/1000), 500, 250, 125, 60, 30, and sometimes 15, 8, 4, 2 (1/2), and 1 second. The B setting is used to make time exposures. Each shutter speed is roughly half or double its immediate neighbor. The shutter will let in half as much light at 1/125 as it will at 1/60 second, but twice as much as if set at 1/250. (Older cameras may have slightly different shutter speeds, such as 500, 200, 100, 50, 25, 15, 10, 5, 2, 1. There's no cause for concern. Operation is exactly the same as with newer values. It might be helpful, however, to have the shutter speeds on an older camera checked for accuracy.)

APERTURE

The aperture controls the *amount* of light you let into the camera. The aperture on most automatic cameras is adjustable from a large opening, *f*/2.8, to a small opening, *f*/22. Contrary to what you'd expect, the *smaller the number, the bigger the aperture.* The *f*-number represents a ratio between the size of the aperture and the focal length of the lens. *f*/11 would mean that the aperture diameter is 1/11 the focal length of the lens. Customary aperture numbers are *f*/22, *f*/16, *f*/11, *f*/8, *f*/5.6, *f*/4, *f*/2.8, *f*/2 and occasionally *f*/1.8, *f*/1.7, or *f*/1.4.

Changing the aperture or the shutter speed will change the amount of light that reaches the film. Automatic cameras will compensate for the gain or loss in light. The picture series at right shows the effect of one-stop changes in the aperture setting. Changing the shutter speed would have produced the same results. Most people would consider the image at lower left to be correctly exposed.

Shutter speed dial

Aperture ring

SHUTTER SPEED PLUS APERTURE

The *f*-numbers work in one sense the same way as shutter speeds. An aperture set at *f*/2.8 lets in twice as much light as its neighbor on the scale, *f*/4, but only half as much as its neighbor on the other side, *f*/2. The big surprise is that the unit spacing for shutter speeds and *f*-numbers is comparable. A change from one shutter speed to the next gives the same exposure result as changing from one *f*-number to the next. This means that several different combinations of *f*-number and shutter speed will give good exposure under the same lighting conditions with the same film. For instance, if you set aperture and shutter speed at *f*/8 and 1/125, respectively, you can get the same exposure as if you had set *f*/5.6 and 1/250, *f*/4 and 1/500, *f*/2.8 and 1/1000, *f*/11 and 1/60, *f*/16 and 1/30, or *f*/22 and 1/15-second.

Fast shutter speed

Slow shutter speed

Large aperture   *Small aperture*

What's the reason for all the numbers? If you think back a second, you'll realize that you need the extensive adjustments to cope with all the possibilities in lighting that you're likely to come across. There are other reasons as well. Fast shutter speeds such as 1/250, 1/500, and 1/1000 will stop rapid action. Slow shutter speeds such as 1/30, 1/15, and 1/8 second are often used intentionally to blur certain action subjects into a swirl of color and motion. Moderate shutter speeds are used for general photography—fast enough to negate hand movement, but slow enough to permit middle-size apertures and medium-speed film.

On the other hand, changing the aperture changes the depth of field (explained in detail on pages 142-143). Large apertures such as $f/2.8$ and $f/2$ give a shallow depth of field where only your subject, or part of your subject, is in sharp focus. Small apertures such as $f/16$ and $f/22$ give great depth of field. Experienced photographers use all these controls—film speed, shutter speed, and aperture size—to keep as much control over the resulting picture as possible.

EXPOSURE METERS

Getting the right exposure for a given situation is often a matter of opinion. Some photographers prefer their slides a little darker than others. Generally, though, acceptable exposure will still show some detail in the brightest areas and some in the darkest.

Most people use manually adjustable cameras with built-in exposure meters or automatic cameras in which a built-in meter sets the shutter speed, the aperture, or both. In any case, the meter will gather the exposure information for you. Always take a reading very close to the subject before stepping back and composing the picture. Check your camera or exposure meter instruction manual for information on its operation.

There are times when a camera exposure meter will not make the right exposure decision. What you must do is recognize the situation and compensate. Here are typical situations and compensations:

Sidelighted subject	increase exposure 1/2 stop
Backlighted subject	increase exposure 1 stop
Small bright subject against dark background	decrease exposure 1 stop
Small dark subject against bright background	increase exposure 1 stop
Average subject in extremely bright scene, such as snow or sand	increase exposure 1 stop

Although camera exposure meters take much of the work out of determining and setting exposure, they often miss in the situations described at left. With an adjustable camera that has a built-in meter, make your meter reading, and then adjust as recommended at left.

On some automatic cameras, there is a way to override manually the automatic exposure feature. It may be a dial that offers up to a two-stop increase or decrease in exposure. It may also be a way to switch the camera to completely manual operation.

Other cameras are entirely automatic with no apparent way to alter the camera-selected settings. To increase the exposure by one stop, set the film-speed indicator to a value half of the speed of the film you're using. To increase exposure by two stops, cut the film speed to one quarter of the real value of the film in the camera. The reverse is true for decreasing exposure. Double the film speed setting for a one-stop decrease in exposure and quadruple it for a two-stop decrease. *DO NOT FORGET TO RETURN THE FILM-SPEED SETTING TO THE CORRECT VALUE AFTER YOU'VE MADE YOUR SPECIAL-SITUATION PICTURE.*

Meter recommendation

Decrease exposure one stop

Meter recommendation

Increase exposure one stop

EXPOSURE SUMMARY

1. Use medium-speed film in normal outdoor situations, high-speed film in dim scenes, and slow-speed film when it's critical that the picture be as sharp as possible.
2. Use a shutter speed at least as fast as 1/125 second for most situations to prevent camera movement from blurring your picture.
3. Fast shutter speeds capture action; slow shutter speeds blur action.
4. Large apertures give shallow depth of field; small apertures give great depth of field.
5. Remember that there are usually several combinations of shutter speed and aperture that will give you correct exposure. Review the reasons for choosing shutter speeds and apertures.
6. Check the manual for your exposure meter or automatic camera to compensate for very bright and very dark subjects.
7. Sidelighting and backlighting often require more exposure than frontlighting—one half and one stop, respectively.

DEPTH OF FIELD

Shallow depth of field—f/2

Great depth of field—f/22

When you focus your camera lens on a subject, you are unknowingly including a greater area in focus. Each aperture setting gives a different depth of field—that is, the distance range that is in acceptably sharp focus. Small apertures such as $f/11$, $f/16$, and $f/22$ give the greatest depth of field, while large apertures such as $f/2.8$, $f/2$, and $f/1.4$ give very little depth of field.

Many single-lens-reflex cameras incorporate a previewer that shows how much of the scene is sharp at different apertures. Other cameras usually include a depth-of-field scale that surrounds the distance scale on the lens barrel. By looking at the indicators for the $f/$number you are using, you can see how much of the scene will be sharp in front of and behind the subject.

Depth of field also depends on the camera-to-subject distance. With the same aperture, depth of field will be shallower if you focus on a nearby object than if you focus on a distant one.

You can include more foreground than background by focusing closer than your main subject but still keeping the subject within the depth of field. The reverse is also true.

You can use your understanding of depth of field to preset your camera in a fast-action situation so that you won't have to refocus as the activity gets close and then recedes. Set the smallest aperture your action shutter speed will allow and then focus on the spot where most of the action will take place. Even if things drift back and forth a little, your pictures will still be in focus.

By aligning the indicators for the aperture setting (f-number) on the depth-of-field scale with the distances on the focusing ring, you can see the range that will be in sharp focus. The aperture above is f/11. The indicators—between 16 and 8 on the depth-of-field scale—show that anything at a distance between 7 and 15 feet from the camera will be in acceptably sharp focus.

With a small aperture and preset focus, you can concentrate on the action.

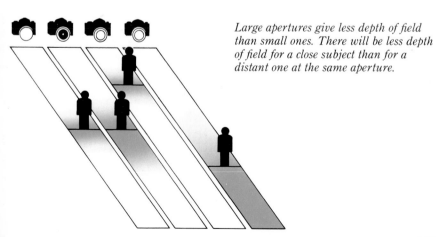

Large apertures give less depth of field than small ones. There will be less depth of field for a close subject than for a distant one at the same aperture.

LIGHTING

Light is the basis for all picture-taking. Light in the morning is a striking change from light at noon. Bright days are vastly different from cloudy days. Shady spots, open fields, and home interiors, summer, fall, winter, and spring all have their unique light properties—all somehow adaptable for good pictures. Let's first discuss the angles of light that apply for almost any situation.

ANGLES OF LIGHT

There are three basic lighting angles—frontlighting, sidelighting, and backlighting. Frontlighting means that light is coming from behind the photographer, brightening the side of the subject facing the photographer. A sidelighted subject has light striking one side, and backlighting illuminates the side of the subject away from the photographer. Frontlighting is common for most picture-taking, but it may not give the most effec-

Frontlighting

Sidelighting

tive photos. People tend to squint when looking into the sun and dark shadows surround their eyes. Frontlighting is also flat, giving few shadows that help create a feeling of perspective.

Sidelighting is more dramatic, with shadows streaking across the picture, helping to establish shape and three-dimensionality. Sidelighting can also give portraits increased impact. Many photographers prefer backlighting for close-up pictures of people, because their subjects never have to look near the sun. Expressions are relaxed and natural and there are no contrasting shadow and lighted areas. Backlighting may also give striking scenic pictures, especially early or late in the day, with long shadows racing back toward the camera from rich, black silhouettes. Sidelighting and backlighting require exposure adjustments for properly exposed subjects (not silhouettes). See page 140-141 in "Exposure" for more information.

Backlighting

IN THE SUN OR OUT

You also have a choice between photographing a subject in bright sunlight or in shade. It depends on the subject. If you want hard, black shadows, photograph in sunlight. If you want a softer quality of light (although a little cooler-colored) take your subject into a shady spot that's clear overhead. There will be plenty of light, but no harshness.

Light overcast days are excellent for some picture-taking. If you have diffused sunlight that creates soft shadows, you have perfect lighting for a portrait.

Bright sun

COPING WITH SUNLIGHT

Sunlight gives shadows. You can reduce the intensity of these shadows by using a crinkled foil or white reflector to bounce light back at the subject. Experiment by angling a white or foil-covered piece of cardboard in different directions to see how much reflection you want.

You can also use light from a flash device to fill in shadows. (See page 158 in "Flash" for more information.)

DIFFERENT TIMES OF DAY

The color and intensity of sunlight changes throughout the day. Early morning photographers (dawn to 9 a.m.) are rewarded with a soft, pale, sometimes rosy light, painting long shadows that

Overcast

Dawn

9 AM

Noon

are freshened by dew. It's beautiful light for land-scapes, especially if you find a few patches of low-lying ground fog. People benefit from this light, too. From 10 a.m. to 4 p.m., sunlight is brilliant and harsh, dropping small, dense shadows. Ordinarily it's not very attractive unless that's the mood you want. From 4 p.m. to sunset, the light deepens in warm tones and lavishly smooths rich shadows across the land. It's dramatic lighting for side-lighted landscapes and sometimes even people. Between sunset and complete darkness comes perfect lighting and color for existing-light city-scapes. (See pages 160-163.)

Without reflector

Bedsheet reflector

INTENSITY

Although our eyes don't see it, there's a vast difference in the intensity of light as it changes. A shaded spot is much darker than a sunlighted area, as is any scene on a cloudy day. Indoors, it's *much* darker than outdoors. (See page 163 in "Existing Light" for more information.) Make sure that you or your camera make the adjustments necessary for changing lighting conditions. (See pages 134-141, "Exposure," and page 131, "Film," for more information about scene brightness.)

Light gives our pictures a chance to appear. It is endlessly variable, and if you study its effects, you'll be able to apply your knowledge to making better pictures in any situation.

With reflector

4 PM

Sunset

SEASONS

As the seasons change, so does the nature of light. Have you ever noticed how much stronger mid-summer light is than spring or winter light? Remember those crisp autumn days when the edges of every leaf seem to snap out toward you? Indeed, the lighting is different. Winter with snow finds the sun at a low angle casting weak shadows, reflecting off snow and ice everywhere. Your meter may be fooled by all the whiteness into recommending underexposure. For snow scenes, increase your exposure one stop (see page 140 in "Exposure") over the meter reading. Springtime also brings weakened sunlight, not reinforced by snow reflections. It's beautiful light for people and other subjects not flattered by strong contrast between shadow and light areas. The sun in summer seems to beat down with a vengeance, almost too strong for most picture-taking. By carefully watching the angles and time of day, you can take endless, excellent pictures in summertime, when all the world comes out to play. Clear, strong (but not overpowering) sunlight characterizes autumn. Brilliant for landscapes, it can also give lovely shade-lighted portraits.

Spring

Summer

Fall

Winter

FLASH

When it's too dark to take pictures, the logical decision is to use flash. Some cameras even tell you when it's necessary. There is nothing tricky about flash photography, provided you know the basics and understand your equipment.

GENERAL TIPS

Reflections Watch out for reflective backgrounds or eyeglasses in the scene. If you take a flash picture directly at either, you'll get an unattractive glare spot in your picture. Stand at an angle to mirrors, windows, or shiny paneling. Ask subjects wearing glasses to turn their heads slightly or remove their glasses.

Reflection in glass

Red Reflections Some people's eyes (and some pets') can reflect flash with an eerie, often red glow. To prevent this internal reflection of the flash, turn on all the room lights—the extra brightness will help reduce the size of the iris. Then, if possible, increase the distance between flash and camera

Change position.

Overexposed foreground   *Foreground objects removed*

lens. Some cameras will accept a flash extender. Finally, back off to a point within the flash range where the reflections will be less noticeable.

Flash Range With snapshot cameras, photograph subjects within the flash range recommended for your camera, flash type, and film. With other cameras, the range for good flash exposure is determined by the film speed, the aperture setting, and possibly the flash mode.

Subjects scattered at different distances.

Overexposed Foreground Any person or object closer than the minimum limit of the flash range will be overexposed and too bright in your flash picture. Compose the scene so that the main subject is closer than anything else, but still within the flash range.

Several Subjects Subjects at different distances from the camera will receive different amounts of flash light—some will be too bright or too dark. Make sure that all your subjects are roughly the same distance from the flash.

Subjects grouped at same distance.

151

SNAPSHOT CAMERAS

To get well-exposed pictures with your snapshot camera, keep your subject in the correct flash distance range—usually 4 to 9 feet with flashcubes, use fresh batteries, and keep the camera-battery contacts clean. With flashcubes, magicubes, or flipflash, check to see that an unused bulb is in position before making an exposure. If you have an add-on or built-in electronic flash unit, see the general information below.

ELECTRONIC FLASH

The most popular flash accessory for 35 mm cameras is the electronic flash unit. Different systems are detailed in the following pages. Before searching for your flash and camera combination, read the general tips below.

1. On a camera with built-in flash, make sure that the film-speed setting is correct for good exposure. Set your film speed on a separate flash unit.

2. If necessary, set the shutter speed recommended by your camera manual for electronic flash. Because the flash duration is typically 1/1000 or less, shutter speed does not affect exposure. If set too fast, however, you'll get partly exposed pictures with a focal-plane shutter or underexposed pictures with a leaf shutter.

3. Focus carefully. Camera-to-subject distance determines exposure with built-in flash.

4. Cameras that don't have built-in flash have an accessory shoe that may be electrically sensitive—a hot shoe. Slide a flash unit with a matching hot foot into the shoe to make the necessary connection. Older cameras or flash units may not be hot. Plug the cord (PC cord) that usually comes with the flash unit into flash and camera. If there is a choice of camera sockets, choose the one marked X—the other is for flashbulbs.

5. Flash units take a few seconds to get ready (recycle) for the next picture. The ready light will glow when the flash is ready. When the ready light takes a long time to glow, change the batteries or recharge the flash unit.

BUILT-IN AND DEDICATED AUTOMATIC

Some 35 mm cameras have a built-in flash unit or can be matched with a special flash unit—a "dedicated" system. Turn on the flash, focus, and take a picture. The camera and flash combination makes exposure settings automatically. Cameras with built-in flash rely on the ISO/ASA speed set on the camera. Separate flash units may need to have the film speed set on a dial.

Press a button to raise and activate the flash.

Other cameras work automatically with any flash, provided that you follow instructions and preset any necessary adjustments, such as flash mode switch or the guide number. (See page 155.) It's necessary to set the focus carefully for sharp pictures *and* for correct exposure. (Focusing also controls the aperture.)

SENSOR-CONTROLLED AUTOMATIC

Automatic flash units designed to work with any camera are governed by light sensors. When you set the ISO/ASA speed on the flash, and select an aperture and a corresponding flash mode, the sensor will govern how much light the flash emits by measuring the intensity of light reflected by the subject. For each aperture and mode combination, the sensor will be able to control flash output over a certain distance range. Read the instruction manual carefully for correct operation of sensor-controlled automatic flash units.

The sensor inside the circle governs flash output.

With a sensor-automatic flash unit, you decide what distance range you'll need, choose the appropriate flash mode, and set the aperture. The flash will do the rest to give good exposure. Make sure to set the film speed on the flash unit. The unit pictured is set at its yellow mode which gives a range of 1.6 to 8.5 feet with an ISO/ASA 100 film at f/8.

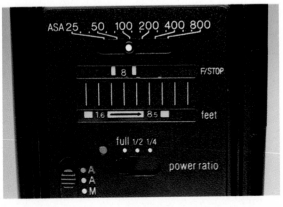

MANUAL FLASH UNITS,
MANUAL OR AUTOMATIC CAMERAS

Older or inexpensive flash units operate at full power for every picture. You have to adjust the camera for correctly exposed flash pictures. Since the shutter speed will always be the same (as recommended by the camera instruction manual— usually 1/30, 1/60, or 1/125 second) you have to set the aperture. Here's a typical operation given in a step-by-step sequence.

1. Attach the flash unit to the camera. If the camera does not have a hot shoe, connect camera and flash with a PC connecting cord*.

1.

2. Set the ISO/ASA speed of the film you're using on the calculator of the flash unit.

2.

3. Set the correct flash shutter speed on the camera.

4. Turn on the flash unit.
5. Focus on your subject.
6. Check the lens distance scale for the distance between flash and subject, assuming that the flash is attached to the camera. (Exposure is always based on the distance between *flash* and *subject*—not camera and subject.)

3.

7. Apply the distance to the flash unit calculator to find the correct aperture.

4.

8. Set the aperture on the camera.
9. Take the picture.

The process usually takes only a few seconds. Many people preset their cameras at 10 feet, particularly at parties and take pictures from that distance only.

5.

6. and 7.

*Older cameras may require you to choose a socket for the PC cord or select a synchronization setting. If faced with a choice of sockets, plug the cord into the socket marked X for electronic flash. The other socket is for a flash-bulb unit. Set a synchronizing switch at X as well. Check your camera manual for additional flash synchronization instructions.

8.

GUIDE NUMBERS

The proliferation of automatic flash systems has nearly erased the memory of a formula used to calculate aperture settings for flash pictures. It may be handy in a pinch.

It works like this. If you know the guide number for your flash unit/film combination, you can easily set the aperture when you know the flash-subject distance. Merely divide the guide number by the distance—the resulting number is the aperture, or very close to it. See the example below.

Guide Number Formula The guide number of the flash unit is 65 with ISO/ASA 100 film. Flash-to-subject distance is 8 feet.

$$65 \div 8 = f/8 \text{ (round when necessary)}$$

Often the guide number for a particular unit is given for only one film speed. Do the same calculations but add or subtract f-stops as indicated by the decrease or increase of speed in the film you're using. (If you're using ISO/ASA 100 film and switch to ISO/ASA 200 film, perform your usual guide number calculation and then select the next smaller f-stop.)

If you need the guide number for a flash unit that has an exposure calculator, set the film speed, and read the guide number across from the 10-foot distance indicator. The guide number changes for different film speeds.

CARE AND HANDLING

An electronic flash unit's worst enemies are weak batteries and infrequency of use. Particularly with rechargeable models that use nickel-cadmium cells, try to take a few flash pictures every month. Better yet, remove and store batteries in the freezer to preserve their life and protect the flash unit's contacts. Remove the batteries with the power on and the capacitor fully charged to protect the flash unit during storage. Before taking pictures after storage, allow frozen batteries several hours of thawing time to reach room temperature. Then, put them in the unit and form the capacitor by firing the flash manually several times. Remember that weak batteries can shorten the life of your flash unit, and it should enjoy a long life.

Replace batteries as recommended. Extend their useful life by occasionally cleaning the contacts with a pencil eraser.

FLASH OFF CAMERA

Moving the flash off the camera flatters many subjects. The lighting gives enough shadow for a three-dimensional appearance.

Removing the flash from the camera may defeat the automatic function of a dedicated flash system. If so, determine exposure by using the manual method described on page 154. Most sensor-

Flash on camera

operated automatic units will perform if the sensor is aimed at the subject, and certainly most manual units will work. All you need is an extension PC cord to connect camera and flash. Remember that *flash-to-subject distance* determines aperture setting. It won't be very different if you hold the unit at arm's length. But if a friend or family member holds the flash unit at a distance different from the camera-subject distance, make your exposure adjustments based on *flash-to-subject* distance.

Flash off camera

BOUNCE FLASH

Bouncing the flash off the ceiling or a nearby wall is another way to improve your subject's appearance. The indirect light is softer, less harsh, and often the soft shadows can help you create a feeling of three-dimensional form.

Again, the idea and execution are fairly simple. Some sensor-governed automatic units will work correctly, provided that the sensor is aimed at your subject. If this is impossible, operate the unit manually, as you will have to do with some

Direct flash

dedicated automatic flash units or a manual unit. Here's how.

Choose a location near a white or light-neutral colored wall or ceiling. The wall may be preferable because it won't cast shadows under a person's eyes. Calculate the distance that the light must travel from flash-to-wall-to-subject. Estimate the aperture necessary for that distance and then open up the aperture an additional two *f*-stops. For instance, let's say that the distance is 15 feet (7 feet from flash to wall and 8 feet back to the subject) and your flash calculator recommends an aperture of *f*/5.6. Instead of *f*/5.6, set *f*/2.8 on the aperture ring.

Your wall and ceiling situations are unique. It's a wise idea to experiment a little with slide film and keep records to fine tune your exposure.

Bounce flash

FILL-IN FLASH

One way to reduce the contrast of shadow and lighted areas in bright sunlight is to fill those shadows with light from an electronic flash unit. (The results may also be satisfactory with a snapshot camera. Try it and see.)

Manual and Sensor-Governed Units The idea is to add a hint of light to a subject in frontlighting, sidelighting, backlighting, or even in the shade. Too much flash light may make your picture appear artificial. Follow these simple guidelines for most manual and sensor-governed automatic flash units.

1. Set the shutter speed recommended for flash photography. Set the aperture for the prevailing lighting conditions with that shutter speed.
2. Set the calculator on your manual or sensor-governed automatic flash unit to a number two or three times as great as the speed of the film you're using. This way the flash will not overpower existing-lighting conditions.
3. Locate yourself and your subject at the distance recommended on the flash calculator for the aperture already set on the camera.
4. Take a flash picture.

Dedicated Automatic Flash Fill On cameras with built-in flash units, just extend the flash and take a picture. There isn't much you can control. Try taping a layer of white tissue over the flash to soften the light. Because cameras that have matched, separate flash units vary in their approach to fill-in flash, read the instructions for your outfit carefully. Make sure you don't cover the sensor with tissue.

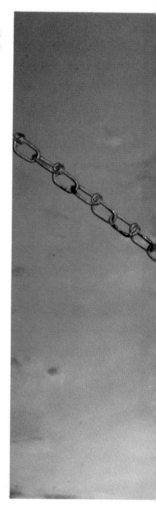

ACTION

The duration of an electronic flash is usually much shorter than your fastest shutter speed. This high-speed capability can stop even very fast action in dark places—children playing, pets jumping, Ping-Pong players smashing, and so on. Exposure is based on flash-to-subject distance. Remember that bounce flash provides more natural light.

Flash is a useful tool that will serve you in many more ways than merely brightening dark interiors. Fill-in flash will brighten the shaded side of a subject outdoors which allows people to look away from the sun. They can relax their faces and eyes from squinting and offer more cheerful, natural expressions. Flash can also stop fast action for a picture, as in the case of the swinging child above.

EXISTING LIGHT

Taking pictures by existing light means picture-taking in dim lighting without flash. You need high-speed film (ISO/ASA 160 to ISO/ASA 400) and a lens with an $f/2.8$ maximum aperture or larger. Read the following pointers and have a look at the exposure suggestions on page 163.

Take exposure meter readings as close to your subject as possible. Avoid reading parts of the scene that include a bright light source, such as this candle. The small spot of bright light may confuse your exposure meter into recommending underexposure.

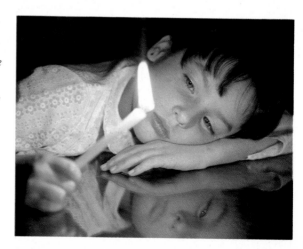

SOME POINTERS

1. Don't include a bright light source when making a meter reading. The light will fool your meter into recommending underexposure.
2. Make meter readings close to your subject.
3. With an automatic camera, get as close as possible to your subject to take the picture.
4. The side of your subject facing the light should probably be the one you photograph.
5. Since your shutter speeds may be fairly slow—often at 1/30 second—hold your camera steady.
6. If you use a shutter speed slower than 1/30 second, brace your camera against something solid or mount it on a tripod.
7. Try to match your film to the scene lighting. Using filters reduces the light available.

8. KODAK EKTACHROME Films and equivalents can be push-processed one additional stop by your photofinisher. If you're using an ISO/ASA 400 film, you can set the film speed dial at ISO/ASA 800 when you ask for special (push) processing. The whole roll must be exposed at the same film speed.

9. A wide range of exposures may be acceptable in many existing-light situations. Experiment with different exposures to see what you prefer.
10. At the very large apertures you'll be using (f/2.8 or f/2), depth of field is very shallow. (See pages 142-143 for more on depth of field.) Make sure to focus carefully.
11. Consult the "Suggested Exposures" table on page 163.

Many existing-light scenes can be captured with a wide range of exposures, as you see in these views of Niagara Falls. It's wise, in fact, to take several pictures at different exposure settings, so that you'll have several to choose from. Left: 2 seconds at f/4, ASA 800. Top left: 4 seconds at f/4, ASA 800. Top right: 8 seconds at f/4, ASA 800.

Suggested Exposures Consider the exposure settings shown at right as guidelines. It's wise to bracket your exposures, especially with slide film, because many existing-light scenes can fool an automatic camera or built-in exposure meter. Typical existing-light subjects may be acceptable in a wide range of exposures.

☐ *For color pictures, use tungsten film. You can use daylight film, but your pictures will look yellow-red.*

☐ *For color pictures, use daylight film or tungsten film with No. 85B filter and 1 stop more exposure.*

☐ *For color pictures, use either daylight or tungsten film.*

In a window-light portrait like this, you'll probably get best results when you take your exposure reading from the bright side of your subject's face. Emphasize that side when you compose the picture.

Suggested Exposures

Picture Subject	ISO/ASA 64–100*	ISO/ASA 125–200	ISO/ASA 400	ISO/ASA 800
AT HOME				
Home interiors at night				
Areas with bright light	$1/15$ sec $f/2$	$1/30$ sec $f/2$	$1/30$ sec $f/2.8$	$1/30$ sec $f/4$
Areas with average light	$1/4$ sec $f/2.8$	$1/15$ sec $f/2$	$1/30$ sec $f/2$	$1/30$ sec $f/2.8$
Candlelighted close-ups	$1/4$ sec $f/2$	$1/8$ sec $f/2$	$1/15$ sec $f/2$	$1/30$ sec $f/2$
Indoor and outdoor holiday lighting at night, Christmas trees	1 sec $f/4$	1 sec $f/5.6$	$1/15$ sec $f/2$	$1/30$ sec $f/2$
OUTDOORS AT NIGHT				
Brightly lighted downtown street scenes (Wet streets add interesting reflections.)	$1/30$ sec $f/2$	$1/30$ sec $f/2.8$	$1/60$ sec $f/2.8$	$1/60$ sec $f/4$
Brightly lighted nightclub or theatre districts—Las Vegas or Times Square	$1/30$ sec $f/2.8$	$1/30$ sec $f/4$	$1/60$ sec $f/4$	$1/125$ sec $f/4$
Neon signs and other lighted signs	$1/30$ sec $f/4$	$1/60$ sec $f/4$	$1/125$ sec $f/4$	$1/125$ sec $f/5.6$
Floodlighted buildings, fountains, monuments	1 sec $f/4$	$1/2$ sec $f/4$	$1/15$ sec $f/2$	$1/30$ sec $f/2$
Skyline—distant view of lighted buildings at night	4 sec $f/2.8$	1 sec $f/2$	1 sec $f/2.8$	1 sec $f/4$
Skyline—10 minutes after sunset	$1/30$ sec $f/4$	$1/60$ sec $f/4$	$1/60$ sec $f/5.6$	$1/125$ sec $f/5.6$
Fairs, amusement parks	$1/15$ sec $f/2$	$1/30$ sec $f/2$	$1/30$ sec $f/2.8$	$1/60$ sec $f/2.8$
Fireworks—displays on the ground	$1/30$ sec $f/2.8$	$1/30$ sec $f/4$	$1/60$ sec $f/4$	$1/60$ sec $f/5.6$
Fireworks—aerial displays (Keep shutter open on Bulb for several bursts.)	$f/8$	$f/11$	$f/16$	$f/22$
Burning buildings, campfires, bonfires	$1/30$ sec $f/2.8$	$1/30$ sec $f/4$	$1/60$ sec $f/4$	$1/60$ sec $f/5.6$
Night football, baseball, racetracks†	$1/30$ sec $f/2.8$	$1/60$ sec $f/2.8$	$1/125$ sec $f/2.8$	$1/250$ sec $f/2.8$
Niagara Falls				
White lights	15 sec $f/5.6$	8 sec $f/5.6$	4 sec $f/5.6$	4 sec $f/8$
Light-colored lights	30 sec $f/5.6$	15 sec $f/5.6$	8 sec $f/5.6$	4 sec $f/5.6$
Dark-colored lights	30 sec $f/4$	30 sec $f/5.6$	15 sec $f/5.6$	8 sec $f/5.6$
INDOORS IN PUBLIC PLACES				
Basketball, hockey, bowling	$1/30$ sec $f/2$	$1/60$ sec $f/2$	$1/125$ sec $f/2$	$1/125$ sec $f/2.8$
Stage shows				
Average	$1/30$ sec $f/2$	$1/30$ sec $f/2.8$	$1/60$ sec $f/2.8$	$1/125$ sec $f/2.8$
Bright	$1/60$ sec $f/2.8$	$1/60$ sec $f/4$	$1/125$ sec $f/4$	$1/250$ sec $f/4$
Circuses				
Floodlighted acts	$1/30$ sec $f/2$	$1/30$ sec $f/2.8$	$1/60$ sec $f/2.8$	$1/125$ sec $f/2.8$
Spotlighted acts (carbon-arc)	$1/60$ sec $f/2.8$	$1/125$ sec $f/2.8$	$1/250$ sec $f/2.8$	$1/250$ sec $f/4$
Ice shows				
Floodlighted acts	$1/30$ sec $f/2.8$	$1/60$ sec $f/2.8$	$1/125$ sec $f/2.8$	$1/250$ sec $f/2.8$
Spotlighted acts (carbon-arc)	$1/60$ sec $f/2.8$	$1/125$ sec $f/2.8$	$1/250$ sec $f/2.8$	$1/250$ sec $f/4$
Interiors with bright fluorescent light	$1/30$ sec $f/2.8$	$1/30$ sec $f/4$	$1/60$ sec $f/4$	$1/60$ sec $f/5.6$
School—stage and auditorium	–	$1/15$ sec $f/2$	$1/30$ sec $f/2$	$1/30$ sec $f/2.8$
Church interiors—tungsten light	1 sec $f/5.6$	$1/15$ sec $f/2$	$1/30$ sec $f/2$	$1/30$ sec $f/2.8$
Stained-glass windows, daytime— photographed from inside	Use 3 stops more exposure than for the outdoor lighting conditions.			

*With ISO/ASA 25-32 film, increase exposure by 1 stop.

†When lighting is provided by mercury-vapor lamps, use daylight film.

FILTERS

Photographers use filters for a variety of reasons. With color film, filters can enhance or diminish effects of lighting color. They can also correct the color of light for film of a particular balance. (See "Film," page 132.) Haze and reflections can be diminished and saturation of colors can be increased with a polarizing filter. Deep color filters primarily used for black-and-white film can be used for special effects with color film. With black-and-white film, filters can increase contrast, correct tonal relationships, reduce haze, and control reflections.

Many glass-mounted filters are available that will screw directly into the front of your lens.

Other filters are available as acetate squares. The squares fit into special frames.

The frames screw into the front of your lens, and can be adapted for a number of lens sizes.

Without polarizer

With polarizer

COLOR FILM

Polarizer The polarizing filter reduces reflections from airborn moisture in the sky (haze) and from non-metallic sources. This means that sky, grass, and other subjects will show more accurate, richer colors. Aim your camera at a 90-degree angle (approximately) to the rays of light for maximum effect. You may also adjust the effect on most polarizing filters by turning the outer filter ring. A polarizing filter always requires a 1⅓-stop exposure increase. Adjust an automatic camera manually because the meter may not give correct exposure.

Polarizers will reduce reflections from non-metallic surfaces such as glass and water. You can control how much reflection you eliminate by operating the adjusting ring on the filter. You may want to retain some sparkle in water scenes.

Without polarizer

With polarizer

Color Correction Filters In the section on "Film," page 132, we discussed films with different color balance. It's convenient if the film in your camera always matches the light where you're photographing. When it doesn't, you can attach the appropriate filter. See the table at right for possible film, light, and filter combinations. Notice also that the table gives exposure adjustment information. Since all filters block some of the light entering the camera, you must always give extra exposure. Operate your camera manually if possible. Meter the scene without a filter attached, make the necessary adjustment, and then add the filter for your picture. (This may not be necessary with through-the-lens metering.) One note here—typical household lighting is tungsten 2850 K. There are also special lights for photography called photolamps 3200 K and 3400 K which require a different film and slightly different filters.

Table Instructions

Conversion filters change the color quality of a light source to match the quality of the light for which a color film is balanced. The table at right shows which filter to use with various film and light combinations. The table also shows how much additional exposure to give for the filters listed.

Tungsten light, daylight film, no filter.

Add a No. 80A filter for correct color.

Conversion Filters for KODAK Color Films

KODAK Color Films	Balanced for	Filter and f-Stop Change		
		Daylight	Photolamp (3400 K)	Tungsten (3200 K)
KODACOLOR II	Daylight, Blue Flash, or Electronic Flash	No filter	No. 80B + 1⅔ stops	No. 80A + 2 stops
KODACOLOR 400		No filter	*No. 80B + 1⅔ stops	*No. 80A + 2 stops
KODACHROME 25 (Daylight)		No filter	No. 80B + 1⅔ stops	No. 80A + 2 stops
KODACHROME 40−5070 (Type A)	Photolamps (3400 K)	No. 85 + ⅔ stop	No filter	No. 82A + ⅓ stop
KODACHROME 64 (Daylight) and EKTACHROME 64 (Daylight)	Daylight, Blue Flash, or Electronic Flash	No filter	No. 80B + 1⅔ stops	No. 80A + 2 stops
EKTACHROME 200 (Daylight)		No filter	No. 80B + 1⅔ stops	No. 80A + 2 stops
EKTACHROME 400 (Daylight)		No filter	No. 80B + 1⅔ stops	No. 80A + 2 stops
EKTACHROME 160 (Tungsten)	Tungsten (3200 K)	No. 85B + ⅔ stop	No. 81A + ⅓ stop	No filter

Note: Increase exposure by the amount shown in the table.   *For critical use.

Daylight, tungsten film, no filter.

Add a No. 85B filter for correct color.

Fluorescent light, daylight film, no filter.   *Add a CC30M filter.*

The table at right gives recommendations for fluorescent light. You'll get best results on color negative film for prints. If you're unsure about bulb type, use the average filter combination. These filters are supplied as 3-inch acetate squares. Glass averaging filters in screw-in mounts are also available. FLD denotes an averaging filter for fluorescent light with daylight film and FLB or FLT works with tungsten film and fluorescent light.

Table Instructions

You can correct color rendition with fluorescent light by using CC (Color Compensating) filters over the camera lens. The table at right tells you which filters to use and how much you have to increase the exposure to compensate for the light absorbed by the filters.

Open shade, no filter.   *Add a No. 81A filter.*

KODAK Color Compensating Filter (CC) for Fluorescent Light

Type of Fluorescent Lamp	KODAK Color Film		
	Daylight		Tungsten
	KODACHROME 25 EKTACHROME 200 KODACOLOR II KODACOLOR 400*	KODACHROME 64 EKTACHROME 64 EKTACHROME 400	EKTACHROME 160
Daylight	40M + 40Y + 1 stop	50M + 50Y + 1½ stops	No. 85B + 40M + 30Y + 1⅔ stops
White	20C + 30M + 1 stop	40M + ⅔ stop	60M + 50Y + 1⅔ stops
Warm White	40C + 40M + 1½ stops	20C + 40M + 1 stop	50M + 40Y + 1 stop
Warm White Deluxe	60C + 30M + 2 stops	60C + 30M + 2 stops	10M + 10Y + ⅔ stop
Cool White	30M + ⅔ stop	40M + 10Y + 1 stop	60R 1⅔ stops
Cool White Deluxe	20C + 10M + ⅔ stop	20C + 10M + ⅔ stop	20M + 40Y + ⅔ stop
Average Fluorescent†	10C + 20M + ⅔ stop	30M + ⅔ stop	50M + 50Y + 1 stop

Note: Increase exposure by the amount shown in the table.　　*For critical use.

†These filters yield less-than-optimum results. Use them only when you can't determine fluorescent lamp type.

There are filters that can warm or cool your color picture slightly. Intended for professional use to get precise matches of film and lighting, they can be very handy for a subject in the blue light of open shade or the fiery light of sunset.

Sunset, no filter.　　　　*Add a No. 82A filter.*

Creative Colors The filters used for black-and-white photography come in a wealth of rich hues. Sometimes one of these can make a brilliant addition to your color pictures. Naturally, blue filters make your pictures blue, and red filters make them red. Exposure is a matter of personal prefer-

No filter   *Yellow filter*   *Orange filter*

ence. Normally it's wise to increase the exposure slightly, but not as much as recommended for correct exposure with that filter and black-and-white film. Experiment a little to see how you like the effects best.

Red filter   *Green filter*   *Deep blue filter*

BLACK-AND-WHITE FILM

Black-and-white film records all colors in many tones of gray—from black through countless grays to white. Subjects that appear nearly white in prints have received a great deal of exposure; dark subjects not nearly as much. Filters transmit their own color of light and subtract others, depending on their color and density. A red flower photographed through a red filter will be nearly white, and the green leaves very dark gray.

Exposure Filters for black-and-white film require exposure compensation. See the table at right for filter and exposure recommendations.

Table Instructions
The table at right shows typical uses for filters with black-and-white film. To apply the exposure information, meter the scene without a filter, make the necessary exposure change, attach the filter, and take the picture.

Color film

Black-and-white film, no filter

Black-and-white film, No. 8 yellow filter

Black-and-white film, No. 25 red filter

Black-and-white film, No. 25 red filter and polarizer

Filters can help bring out striking contrasts in black-and-white landscape photos. A No. 8 yellow filter gives the scene a tonal rendition similar to the color version. A red or polarizing filter will heighten the contrast. Adding the red filter to the polarizer makes the scene even more dramatic.

172

Filter Recommendations for Black-and-White Films

Subject	Effect Desired	Suggested Filter	Increase Exposure by:
Blue Sky	Natural	No. 8 Yellow	1 stop
	Darkened	No. 15 Deep Yellow	1½ stops
	Spectacular	No. 25 Red	3 stops
	Almost black	No. 29 Deep Red	4 stops
	Night effect	No. 25 Red, plus polarizing screen	4½ stops
Marine Scenes When Sky Is Blue	Natural	No. 8 Yellow	1 stop
	Water dark	No. 15 Deep Yellow	1½ stops
Sunsets	Natural	None or No. 8 Yellow	1 stop
	Increased brilliance	No. 15 Deep Yellow or No. 25 Red	1½ or 3 stops
Distant Landscapes	Addition of haze for atmospheric effects	No. 47 Blue	2⅔ stops
	Very slight addition of haze	None	None
	Natural	No. 8 Yellow	1 stop
	Haze reduction	No. 15 Deep Yellow	1½ stops
	Greater haze reduction	No. 25 Red or No. 29 Deep Red	3 or 4 stops
Nearby Foliage	Natural	No. 8 Yellow or No. 11 Yellowish-Green	1 or 2 stops
	Light	No. 58 Green	2⅔ stops
Outdoor Portraits Against Sky	Natural	No. 11 Yellowish-Green No. 8 Yellow, or polarizing screen	2, 1, or 1½ stops
Flowers—Blossoms and Foliage	Natural	No. 8 Yellow or No. 11 Yellowish-Green	1 or 2 stops
Red, "Bronze," Orange, and Similar Colors	Lighter to show detail	No. 25 Red	3 stops
Dark Blue, Purple, and Similar Colors	Lighter to show detail	None or No. 47 Blue	None or 2⅔ stops
Foliage Plants	Lighter to show detail	No. 58 Green	2⅔ stops
Architectural Stone, Wood, Fabrics, Sand, Snow, etc, When Sunlit and Under Blue Sky	Natural	No. 8 Yellow	1 stop
	Enhanced texture rendering	No. 15 Deep Yellow or No. 25 Red	1½ or 3 stops
Interiors in Tungsten Light	Natural	No. 11 Yellowish-Green	2 stops

Contrast and Separation One of the main uses for filters in black-and-white photography is to separate subjects of different colors into strikingly different tones. Black-and-white film may see the red tones and the blue tones as nearly equal. A red filter will make the red tones white and the blue tones dark. A blue filter, however, will make the blue tones lighter and the reds dark. See the examples at right.

Use color filters to separate tones in black-and-white pictures. In the comparison at right, note the different values given to the red and blue areas by the red and blue filters.

Color correction Black-and-white film is affected by different qualities of light. Tungsten light is much redder than sunlight. A yellow-green filter can help the film render the correct tonal relationships in a scene lighted by tungsten light.

Polarizer A polarizing filter will also help reduce haze and reflection in black-and-white pictures while increasing contrast. The guidelines for handling and exposure adjustment are the same as for color film. (See page 165.)

Filters can increase contrast between sky and clouds.

Color film

Black-and-white film, no filter

Black-and-white film, red filter

Black-and-white film, blue filter

LENSES

If you have a camera that accepts interchangeable lenses—typically a single-lens-reflex—the following information is devoted to lens talk.

The lens that came on your camera is probably a normal lens. Normal means that it sees perspective, image size, and distance relationships about the same as your naked eye. It is very likely a fast lens with an $f/2.8$ or larger maximum aperture. Normal lenses are designed for general picture-taking—the kind most of us do around the home, on vacation, and at special events. Other lenses have special features that make them ideally suited for certain kinds of photography.

TELEPHOTO LENSES

Telephoto lenses make a subject look bigger than it is—just like a telescope or a pair of binoculars. It doesn't show as much of the scene as a normal lens, but what's there is brought in close. The strength of a telephoto lens is determined by its focal length—an optical measurement. Your normal lens (on a 35 mm camera) is roughly 50 mm (2 inches) long. A 100 mm telephoto lens will give 2X magnification

Telephoto lens

and a 200 mm lens 4X magnification. What you give up for the increased image size is: cost—telephotos can be rather expensive; weight—they're bigger and heavier than normal lenses; speed—telephoto lenses have smaller maximum apertures than normal lenses, and depth of field—at the same aperture, a telephoto lens gives much shallower depth of field than a normal lens.

Telephoto lenses command some special provinces. Most photographers prefer to take portraits with a moderate telephoto lens (75 to 135 mm for a 35 mm camera). It allows a large image without getting too close to the subject. Since the perspective is slightly different, there is little distortion of the subject's features, such as you would find with a normal lens at close distances. And because depth of field is shallow, it's easy to focus on the subject with a fairly large aperture and throw the background into an unobtrusive blur. Stronger telephoto lenses—200 mm and more—can help you get

500 mm telephoto lens

200 mm telephoto lens

100 mm telephoto lens

50 mm normal lens

closer to sports, wildlife, and other distant subjects when you can't approach physically. An important note here—telephoto lenses require faster shutter speeds to eliminate blurry pictures caused by camera movement. Some photographers round off the reciprocal of the focal length of the lens (one divided by the focal length) to determine the best shutter speed. A 200 mm lens would need a shutter speed of at least 1/250 second. If this isn't possible, steady the camera on a solid support such as a tripod, table, or wall.

WIDE-ANGLE LENSES
As the name implies, wide-angle lenses see more of a scene than normal or telephoto lenses. The subject will also be smaller than with a normal lens. Wide-angle lenses give great depth of field. They're also fairly small, except for the extreme wide-angle lenses, and fairly fast. They're also more expensive.

35 mm wide-angle lens

28 mm wide-angle lens

24 mm wide-angle lens

16 mm wide-angle lens

Wide-angle lens

Some situations demand wide-angle photography. Building interiors and narrow streets would limit a normal lens. But with a wide angle you'll get much more of the scene. Be careful with people and buildings because perspective changes with wide-angle lenses. Faces can be distorted when too close. Bodies can look like a side show attraction. If you tilt your camera up too far, a building will appear to be falling backwards.

Moderate wide angles—28 to 35 mm—are very useful. Some photographers consider them to be normal lenses. Very wide-angle lenses—18 to 25 mm—are much more extreme and generally used for special applications or to amplify distortion.

ZOOM LENSES

Modern zoom lenses allow you a range of focal lengths—extreme wide angle to moderate wide angle, moderate wide angle to normal, moderate wide angle to moderate telephoto, and moderate

180

Macro lens

telephoto to strong telephoto. They're usually a bit heavier and costlier than single-focal-length lenses, but they're incredibly versatile, especially when you are traveling. Instead of packing a whole bag of lenses, you might take only two—a 35-to-85 mm zoom and an 80-to-200 mm zoom. All you have to do is adjust the focal length until the scene looks right in the viewfinder.

MACRO LENSES
Macro, or rather close-focusing lenses, are designed to give their sharpest images of very close subjects. People who specialize in close-ups of flowers, insects, and other small subjects will cheerfully pay the bill for this specialized piece of equipment. Some zoom telephoto lenses have close-focusing capability when set in the macro or close-focus mode.

CLOSE-UPS

With many cameras, you can usually find a way to isolate small subjects such as a single big flower or a tidy group of lesser blossoms. The easiest way is with an accessory called a close-up lens, which allows you to get closer than the minimum focusing distance for your camera. More advanced cameras have a threaded connector at the end of the lens where you can screw in close-up lenses or filters. Less advanced cameras might require you to tape a close-up lens over the camera lens.

Close-up lenses come graded in diopters—typically +1, +2, and +3. The higher the number, the closer you can get, and the bigger your image will be. If you have a camera that has a viewfinder separate from the lens, it might be best to use only one close-up lens, a +2 for instance, so that you get completely familiar with how it works. (As you'll see later, close-up lenses require a little measuring and calculation for accurate results.) A single-lens-reflex camera, however, shows you in the viewfinder almost exactly what will be on the film, so you can use any close-up lens, or even a combination of close-up lenses for the best treatment of your subject.

The viewfinder for any rangefinder camera is adjusted to give you accurate framing (you get what you see) from the minimum focusing distance to infinity. At the closer distances you'll use with a close-up lens, the viewfinder will not show exactly what the film will record. And, since depth of field is so shallow at close focusing distances, you'll want the camera lens to be at the precise distance recommended by the close-up lens instruction sheet or in the table on page 185. To aim your camera from the correct distance, attach a string to the camera with a knot tied at the recommended distance. Extend the string until the knot just touches the subject. Then you're at the right distance. When you hold the string out, make sure the camera lens is pointed directly at the subject. Then drop the string and snap the picture. With practice, this becomes a simple and effective way to make close-ups.

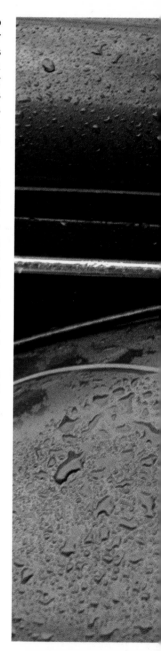

Almost as easy, and much more accurate is a lightweight cardboard measuring device. Cut to the recommended distance, the board should have a lengthwise line at center that you line up from camera lens to subject. The board should be only as wide as the long dimension of the field of view for that close-up lens. That way, you'll know how much of the subject will be included in the picture. Make sure the camera isn't tilted up or down, remove the cardboard, and take your picture.

Cardboard measuring device

Shown below is information you'll want to use for taking close-up pictures with a rangefinder camera. The left column shows different close-up lenses and lens combinations at various camera lens focus settings. The next column gives lens-to-subject distances for you to measure. The columns on the right give the field size (subject area) for the combinations shown at left. Just remember to measure the distance carefully from the front rim of your close-up lens to the subject. Aim the camera lens directly at the subject. Incidentally, close-up lenses require no exposure compensation.

Close-Up Lens Data

Close-up Lens and Focus Setting (in feet)		Lens-to-Subject Distance (in inches)	Approximate Field Size (in inches)	
			38–40 mm Lens on a 35 mm Camera	50 mm Lens on a 35 mm Camera
+1	Inf	39	23⅛ x 34½	18 x 27
	15	32¼	18⅞ x 28⅛	14⅝ x 21⅞
	6	25½	14⅝ x 21¾	11⅜ x 16⅞
	3½	20⅜	11½ x 17⅛	8⅞ x 13¼
+2	Inf	19½	11⅝ x 17¼	9 x 13½
	15	17¾	10⅜ x 15½	8 x 12
	6	15½	8⅞ x 13¼	6⅞ x 10¼
	3½	13⅜	7⅝ x 11⅜	5⅞ x 8¾
+3	Inf	13⅛	7¾ x 11½	6 x 9
	15	12¼	7⅛ x 10⅝	5½ x 8¼
	6	11⅛	6⅜ x 9½	5 x 7⅜
	3½	10	5⅝ x 8½	4⅜ x 6½
+3 plus +1	Inf	9⅞	5¾ x 8⅝	4½ x 6¾
	15	9⅜	5½ x 8⅛	4¼ x 6⅜
	6	8⅝	5 x 7⅜	3⅞ x 5¾
	3½	8	4½ x 6¾	3½ x 5¼
+3 plus +2	Inf	7⅞	4⅝ x 6⅞	3⅝ x 5⅜
	15	7½	4⅜ x 6½	3⅜ x 5⅛
	6	7⅛	4⅛ x 6⅛	3⅛ x 4¾
	3½	6⅝	3¾ x 5⅝	2⅞ x 4⅜
+3 plus +3	Inf	6⅝	3⅞ x 5¾	3 x 4½
	15	6⅜	3¾ x 5½	2⅞ x 4¼
	6	6	3½ x 5⅛	2⅝ x 4
	3½	5⅝	3¼ x 4¾	2½ x 3¾

Attaching +1 close-up lens

CAMERA CARE

Although a precision instrument, your camera is designed for hard use. It does deserve whatever care you can provide. Here are some guidelines:

1. Protect your camera from dirt and bumps with a ready case.
2. Keep the inside clean by using a soft brush or air syringe at film-change time. You can also use canned compressed air, but follow instructions on the can or in your camera instruction manual carefully. Misuse could damage your camera. Also, aim the air stream precisely—it's possible to blow debris *into* the camera.
3. Keep the lens protected from dirt and fingerprints with a lens cap.
4. Clean the lens by first brushing or blowing off surface debris. Then use photographic lens tissue (not the kind for eyeglasses) and a drop or two of lens cleaning fluid to wipe off smudges.
5. Protect your camera from water—particularly

1. Use a camera case.

2. Keep the camera clean.

3. Protect the lens.

4. Clean the lens.

5. Shield your camera.

6. Change the batteries.

7. Remove for storing.